Enemies of the Human Soul

Enemies of the Human Soul

Fritz Bazin

ISBN: 1-58721-573-X

1stBooks – rev. 1/25/01

About the Book

The book is one of the most powerful piece materials carefully prepared, to help christians who have the desire to go deeper in the Word of God. Those who are not satisfied just being religious, but who want to grow spiritually in God. This book will help them to see and understand the bible in a different way. They will understand that the bible is not a natural book. That it takes a spiritual touch from God to understand the word of God. I believe that this book will indeed make a difference, and can even change the life of anybody who takes time to read it carefully. I believe it will help produce some kind of understanding in individuals who really care for their spiritual life. It's a combination of different subjects that can really help you to understand some great keys in the bible, etc. God had revealed these things to me for a purpose. The purpose is to help open your spiritual eyes, to be able to see things in a different perspective; even better than from what you have previously learned. The greatest mystery in our times is the mystery of ungodliness. These are not some things that anyone can easily know. It takes God himself to reveal these things to different individuals to whom he wishes. There is a big difference between the word of God, and religious philosophies invented by men's carnal minds. Men's religious inventions cannot help your soul to become alive. However, the word of God can! It will help you to begin to see and understand the plan of God, in a better way.

ACKNOWLEDGEMENT

I give all my gratitude to Mary Vital for her talents and her contributions in this work. She did an outstanding job helping to put this book together. Her patience has been extended for this work in a way that I myself sometimes feel embarrassed about. Her input and dedication to this work is greatly appreciated!

Fritz Bazin

TABLE OF CONTENTS

Introduction

From the Author

After 14 years of studies, I feel that it is necessary for me to share my knowledge with the Christian world. God says my people are perished because of their ignorance. Today the greatest problem Christians are facing is the lack of knowledge and understanding of the word of God. This book is a result of years of study and research, put together to help our brothers and sisters in Christ to understand or comprehend the mysteries of the Bible. There are many great teachings out there that are creating more confusion, instead of helping Christians understand the plan of God. I hope this book is a blessing to those who take the time to read it. It will open your eyes to see that the real truth of the word of God. These things had been hidden to the wise men of this age but were revealed to the simple. The Bible is not a literal book that we can read with our intellect only. It takes a spiritual touch to truly understand the Bible. That is why many are dying spiritually, and even physically, because of their ignorance of the things of God. The Pharisees and the Sadducces were great people, always ready to defend what they believe, yet because of their ignorance and pride, they had fallen into a profound spiritual darkness. They were able to produce a crystallization of doctrines that prevented others to enter in the kingdom of God. That is why Jesus told them that they too would not enter in. Jesus called them white tombs, which look like they are good on the outside but they are filthy on the inside. That is what we see in our generation. There are many so-called doctors of divinity when they are so ignorant in the things of God! Because they pretend they know when they know nothing, God lets them fall into great confusion. Most of them call the truth of the word of God lies and they call lies truth. This book is designed to help you understand the plan of God for humanity. Those so-called great religious philosophers are the ones who keep God's people captive with their false doctrines. No one has it all but it takes a humble spirit to understand the things of God. God always deals with men in mysteries. Only those who found His favor would have these things revealed to them. As for those who think they know all the mysteries of God and who even call themselves doctors of divinity, they will die in their ignorance as the Pharisees and the Sadducces died in their sins in 70 A.D. Salvation has three phases not just one phase as is preached in the religious world. In this book you will find that subject; please take the time to read it and carefully examine the scriptures. You will understand it. There are many subjects in this book that I feel they can help you, not only with your spiritual life but also they will open your eyes so that no one will be able to fool you anymore. You will be a strong person, not in the flesh but in God. Many are strong not in spiritual things of God but in the flesh. The greatest mystery today is the mystery of ungodliness. We see those who would need help themselves, are in leadership positions. This is one of the greatest problems we are facing today, blind leading the blind. When Jesus was here on earth, everything he did was a lesson. Everything Jesus taught needs to be carefully re-examined to see what He really meant. That was why the big crowd who was following Jesus never truly understood a thing He was saying. It was because they took Jesus with simplicity. They did not see the depth of the things He was preaching. So are those of our time. I pray that the Lord touches your eyes and helps you understand everything in this book.

God bless you!

Fritz Bazin

The Standards Of The Body Of Christ

How can we become members of the Body of Christ? What are the requirements and how can we achieve each and every one of them? Can we build on the pattern of the primitive church? Building churches and gathering people together in religious activities is one thing. However, to build according to the true pattern of the church that Jesus had built is another thing.

The church of the Body of Christ has standards, and it's only by these standards that you can identify the true church of the Body of Christ. Many may claim that they are building the Body of Christ church, but there will be a time where God will shake every one of them. Then you will know which one is the true Body of Christ. You cannot build without standards. There should be a standards of dress, a standard of behavior, a standard of conversation, and a standard of the attendance and the time we come to church. There should be an exact time to start and every single member should be in his or her spot at that time.

The spirit of God always leads the church of the Body of Christ, not by preset programs. When it is done that way, there is no room for the Holy Spirit to operate freely. The church of the Body of Christ is a place where every member is practicing personal holiness (Rom. 12:1-2). The primary vision of a pastor is to establish a high moral standard and to set a pattern of holiness for everybody to follow. God is a holy God. Anything unholy will not please him (1 Peter 1:15) (1 Thess. 3:13) (1 Thess. 4:7). We cannot just talk or preach about holiness and not pursue holiness. If we believe in something then we should seek it with all of our strengths.

The people of the Body of Christ are a separated people, a people sanctified above any other religious activity on earth. That is why we must walk worthy of our vocation. The church of the Body of Christ is a chaste virgin, not simply a virgin, but a chaste virgin.

This church has a very high spiritual standard that cannot be compared to any other church in the world. To be holy, there must be certain guidelines to follow. We cannot create our own ways to serve God. God has his ways and it's up to us to measure up to them. If we don't, then we will be the losers. If we want to be holy, then we will do our best to eliminate anything that would feed the flesh (Rom. 6:3-4).

Baptism in Christ means death for the worldly things! Jesus said, in Matt. 16:24, "if any man will come to me, let him deny himself and take his cross and follow me." The word cross here means your will and the will of God. If you want to serve God, your own will must be put to death for you to be able to do the will of God. You cannot be following your will and at the same time claim to be a saint of God. The word *deny* is a command. It's a condition that Christ put before us. The only way we can please him as Christians, is to first fulfill that part. The Bible says, in 1 Tim. 2:9, "in like manner also, that women adorn themselves in modest apparel, with shame Facade and sobriety; not with braided hair or gold or pearls or costly array; but which becometh women professing godliness, with good works." Verse 11 says, "let the woman learn in silence with all subjection." These were the standards of the first church. If we want to build upon the same foundations, then we must put these things in execution in our lives. Women in today's church have no standards at all. They come to church with short dresses, almost half-naked. The men are coming to church in short pants and short sleeves, and no one says anything to them; they are welcomed.

The church should be a place only for those who are willing to change. If we call ourselves Christians, and there is nothing in us to differentiate us from the ungodly people of the world, then what kind of Christians are we really? If we come to God, it means that we will follow all of the guidelines and all of his commandments. "Therefore, if any man be in Christ, he is a new creature; old things are become new" (2 Cor. 5:17). If we become new in God, we must walk in spirit (Rom. 6:4). We must walk in the newness of life in Christ. We cannot walk in the newness of life in Christ if we continue to live our lives according to the vanity of this world. "And be not conformed to this world: But be ye transformed by the renewing of your mind, that ye may prove what is that good, and acceptable and perfect will of God" (Rom. 12:2).

The church of the Body of Christ is a spiritual mother for all spiritual new converts in Christ. The old members of the church in general should become like mothers who take care of the new babies in Christ. They should never let a new convert in Christ sit by him or herself. Someone with spiritual maturity should sit next to them to make sure that they fully understand what the pastor is preaching. They should help them to search the scriptures.

Liberalism

The question we ask ourselves today is, can liberal Christians go to Heaven? Can all of those out there claim that they are the followers of Christ when they are living their lives their own way, when they are living like the ungodly without any difference whatsoever? Jesus made a statement in Matt. 16:24-25, "if any man will come to me, let him deny himself first and follow me."

In Matt. 7:13, Jesus shows us two ways: the broad way and the narrow way. The choice is ours to make. Either the broad way, which will lead us to everlasting death or the narrow way, which will lead us to everlasting life. We must bear in mind that the narrow way is not an easy way. It is not a form; it's the real thing, and it's only through the narrow way that we can find Christ. It's only through self-denial that we can find life. The broad way is the way of the world, and that's where most people are directing themselves now. We can see the effect that this has on the path of holiness today. People don't want to practice personal holiness anymore. They want to follow the broad way. They want an easy path to Christianity. They forget the price needed to be paid to enter into the life elements. The narrow way is where the perfect will of God is. That is where Jesus had to go to enter into the fullness of the life elements. Not only did he have life, but also he is able to give life to us. He shows us the source of life, the true eternal and invisible God, the creator of the universe. It is only through the narrow way that we can begin to stimulate everlasting life in our souls.

We see how some Christians are trying to bring paganism back into Christianity again. They had done it in the past and now they are trying their best to bring it back. They are even trying to bring rock music and rap music, with its violent and unacceptable behaviors and pagan rhythms, into Christianity. The question we ask ourselves is, can we fool God, or are we only fooling ourselves? We know for sure that these things are contrary to the standards of God. These things are not of God. Where will these things lead us today? Will these things help our souls to prosper in God, or will they lead us into everlasting death? Some preachers even say that these things are the only way we can save our youth. I say that this is a big lie! We cannot save our youth by conforming to them in their infirmities. The only way we can save them is by taking them away from these things. If we are conforming to the world, what makes us think that we are not the world? In John 2:15 it says, "love not the world, nor the things in the world." If you love the world, the love of God is not in your heart. Television, by example, is a way to bring all the filth of the world into your house. Television is not a source of information anymore. It has become a source of corruption and immorality. If we want to go with God all the way, we must get rid of all of these things in our lives. I know it is not easy to change but we must make a commitment with ourselves not to let these things destroy the spiritual life we have in God. Jesus paid a great price for the spiritual life that he gave us. We must not take it lightly or play with it. If we do, we only condemn our souls.

All liberals will go to hell without the hope of a resurrection. If we leave God's way of life (Jesus) and create our own ways to serve him, we will perish in our sins. God's way is the only way of life, and there is no substitution or short cut in it. There is one way, and that's all. Any other things will lead us to death and that's the reality. Take note that it says in Matt. 7 that only a few found the narrow way. That tells us that the great multitudes are not going to make it, because all of them are already headed for the broad way and that is their destiny.

We must do our best to understand the plan of God. God only reveals his plans through his principles that we will find them, and they are not easy to understand. It is only those who seek them with all their hearts, and in humbleness and supplication. Jesus said, "God hides these things from the wise and the prudent and reveals them to the babies." When we become wise in our own eyes, we will not understand the hidden things of God.

When you go to certain churches, you can plainly see that they create their own heaven, and they rejoice themselves in the flesh and feel very comfortable with it. The spirit of God never touches their hearts. They dwell in spiritual death, without even realizing it. They say they are going to heaven, but you don't know which heaven they are going to, because their ignorant activities blind them from seeing the true will of God. God wants everyone to be saved, but our ignorance can keep us in bondage forever. It is not God's plan for men to have only religious activities, which are not according to his plan. Man always does his best to destroy his own soul, no matter what. We can never make it in the holiest of holy, where God dwells, through our own religious activities. We can only make it through God's ways. We know that God's ways (laws of God) are the ways of life and that man's ways (laws of men) are the ways of death.

The Two Treasures

Most Christians of our time are more concerned about the natural things of the world than seeking for the spiritual things, which cannot perish. In Matt. 6:19-21 Jesus said, "lay not up yourselves treasures upon the earth, where moth and rust doth corrupt, and where thieves break through and steal. But lay up for yourselves treasures in Heaven, where neither moth nor rust doth corrupt and where thieves do not break through nor steal. For where your treasure is, there will your heart be also." What do we consider our treasures to be? The things that dominate your heart the most are considered as treasures. What is the most important thing for you today? Is it your wife, your children or your money? Whatever it is, can it save your soul? When you go to your grave, can these things preserve your soul? If not, then you should reconsider what you make your treasures.

Some people think that having a lot of money in the bank and having good health is all they need to have it made. They don't think they need anything else. The true treasure is when you have heavenly things that can preserve your life; things that can help you remain in the existence in Christ, even after your death. "Seek ye first the kingdom of God, and his righteousness; and all these things shall be added into you" (Matt. 6:33). You must reach a point where you put God first in everything in your life. Verse 34 says, "take therefore no thought for the morrow: for the morrow shall take care of itself." The Bible tells us not to be afraid of what we will eat tomorrow, because fearing what we will become may cause us to do things sometimes that are contrary to the standards of God. When we learn to trust God in everything, then we will begin to see the difference between those who trust God and those who trust in themselves.

God is the supplier of all of our needs. We should not try to compromise or try to trade our spiritual treasures for the natural things of the world. That is why Jesus said that the natural things are temporary, but the invisible things are forever. So we should reconsider where to put our trust today, either in the things of God, which will endure forever, or in the things of the world,

which will perish. Where are your treasures today, in God or in
the world?

The Mystery of Iniquity

Iniquity is one the deepest mysteries to ever exist. When someone finds him or herself in that condition, only God can deliver them. In the time we are now living, iniquity is one of the most destructive tools used to destroy the church. People in such situations never realize that they are on the path of destruction until it happens to them.

They always find ways to justify their actions. They think that no one else is right but them. They are self-righteous and very arrogant. They never have any respect for authority. They also have ways to make people believe in them and cause others to follow them. Preachers can be like that, and saints can be like that, but mostly young leaders can find themselves in such situations. Jealousy and pride are the reasons for it. When they see that God is blessing someone else, they feel that they should be the one in such a position. Knowing that they are not, they rise up against that person. When someone or a group of people becomes like that, they automatically become the enemies of the truth! They will rise against whatever the pastor does or preaches. They will produce their own disciples to back them up in whatever they do or say against the pastor of the church. In the Old Testament, we read how the children of Korah revolted against Moses and how God destroyed them all in the wilderness.

There are two kinds of iniquity. One is when a religious system or a cult teaches certain doctrines that are contrary to the holy doctrine of God. That is iniquity in God's eyes. When someone rises up against a man of God, without any cause, this is also called iniquity, because it destroys the faith of the new babies of Christ, and God hates those who are promoting division in his church.

People who don't want to go all the way with God and block the way for others to enter, and those who don't really want to serve God but want to establish themselves as kings over God's people are also iniquitous. The word iniquity means confusion. When someone is causing confusion among God's people, it's something terrible, because you can receive eternal judgment at any time. When a religious system preaches false doctrine to God's people, it's also a terrible thing. God really hates any cults that teach confusion or cause his people to be confused and lost. That is why it's so important to avoid any cult that preaches false doctrines because it will damn your soul.

Restoration of the Church

How is the church going to be restored? What will it take for that to happen and when will it take place? Many preachers say that the church will be restored when they all have doctrinal harmony, but in reality, it's just a part of the truth, not the whole truth. First of all, it will take a restored ministry to restore the church, and it's going to take a lot to have a restored ministry in our time. Nothing imperfect can possibly produce perfection. It takes the real truth of the word of God to produce full maturity in a people.

There must be a group of men sanctifying themselves to God, one hundred percent, with no reserve. When we observe the lives of some great men of God in the past, we see that these men were willing to lose something in order to apprehend God totally. They were willing to give up their sex lives for the power of the Holy Ghost to work in them without measure. The problem we have today is that no one is willing to give up that part. Until a group of men is willing to lose their sex lives for God, there can never be a restored church or a restored ministry. The Holy Ghost can never freely work in men's lives if they only sanctify their lives partially to God. They must submit their lives totally to gain the fullness of the power of God in their lives. It's true that they need to have doctrinal harmony and one mind to achieve that but it requires much more than that. As long as they keep digging the flesh, they can never receive the fullness of the Holy Ghost in their lives.

When God chose Moses to lead the children of Israel out of Egypt, Moses automatically lost his sex life. When Jesus called the twelve Apostles to become his Disciples, they had also lost their sex lives, as did Paul and many other great men of God. Even the shadows of some of these men could heal the sick. They walked through the sick, and they were all healed.

Why do you think they had such power working in their lives? It was because they had given up their sex lives. The Holy Ghost is a holy spirit. They only way it can work with full strength within us, is when we totally live our lives for God and only God. Our lives must be pure, without any spots. Rev. 14:4 says, "these are which were not defiled with women; for they are virgins. They had followed the lamb withersoever he goeth. These were the redeemed from among men, being first fruit unto God and the lamb." Preachers may spiritualize this verse, but the truth is, those who were not defiled with women are those who found the Lord and were able to keep their personal holiness and walk a very high level of holiness and sanctity before God. They kept themselves pure and holy, without spots. I believe the women spoken about here are natural, not spiritual women. If this is so, then why did the twelve apostles have to give up their sex lives after the day of Pentecost? And why did Paul and so many others who made it to the Bride of Christ, do it also? The life they had before the day of Pentecost was not counted for God. That is the way they had kept their virginity. Their lives began the very first day they received the baptism of the Holy Ghost.

That doesn't mean that those of our day who found the Lord and are striving to live for the Lord will not be saved. This is not what I mean at all. I only refer to those who will be the spiritual government of Christ, those who will be members of the Bride of Christ. Remember that there will be people who will be invited to the Bride, but they will not be the Bride themselves. People are confused about those who will be the Bride and those who will only be invited. Remember in any wedding, there are always people who are invited. They are not themselves the bride. They are only guests. It will be the same for the Bride of Christ.

There will be people who are worthy enough to be invited to the Bride of Christ, but those who will be members of the Bride must meet all the requirements without missing even one.

There will be a restored church in our day. It is going to take place when those who were called of God to partake of his divine nature give up the flesh totally. This is when the restoration will begin. Their lives must be completely submitted to the Holy Spirit. Many speak about the restoration of the church, when they are the ones who keep the church from being restored. Their ignorance keeps them in the dark. This is a great revelation! God will have a judgment seat on the earth to judge this ungodly world, but this will only take place when the ministers give up all the activities of the flesh among them. God is a holy God, and nothing unclean can stand before Him. How can we stand before him when we are still digging the flesh? "And the Lord said unto Moses, go unto the people and sanctify them (away from sex) today and tomorrow, and let them wash their clothes, and be ready against the third day: for the third day the Lord will come down in the sight of all the people upon Mount Sinai. And he said unto the people, be ready against the third day: come not at your wives" (Ex. 19:10-11,15). He is referring to sexual activities here when he says, "come not at your wives." This means that God does not like the idea of his preachers digging the flesh while they are preaching his word.

Hidden Enemies

The hidden are enemies within men's nature before and after conversion! When we came to God, we came as sinners with our Adamic nature. Our souls are attached to the Adamic nature, and we don't really know if we have such a nature in us.

After being converted and received the baptism of the Holy Ghost, with a lot of teaching we become knowledgeable of the word of God. Then we begin to have a war with ourselves, which still wants to be fed. When the Holy Ghost and our inner voice keep reminding us not to do what we are tempted to desire, then the separation begins to take place. Our souls are asking to be fed constantly with the word of God. The old nature is also asking to be fed, that puts us in the position of choosing for ourselves, which one will feed more. As we already know, the Adamic nature is often interpreted as a serpent. It will never give up. It will constantly ask to be fed. We must have enough courage to deny it of all it wants. If not, we will never reach spiritual maturity. If we never reach spiritual maturity, we cannot be completely saved. When we become knowledgeable of the word of God, we become more exposed to all kinds of temptations. If we are not very strong, we could find ourselves doing things that are contrary to the law of God.

When you have enemies, you must first locate where they hide. Once you know their hiding place then you must have a plan to destroy them all. If we don't destroy our enemies, then they will destroy us. We must know that our enemies are within us. We don't have to look anywhere else for them because they are within us. All desires that are contrary to the law of God are our enemies!

Jesus, who was the Son of God, knew that his true enemy was the desire not to obey the law of God. So he diligently fought the desire and overcame it by prayer and fasting.

Today's Christians don't like to pray, and I won't even mention fasting because it's something that doesn't even exist for some of today's Christians. They are too busy taking care of their natural needs, so they neglect their souls. If Jesus saw the necessity to do these things, then how can we neglect them?

Certain desires can only be overcome by fasting, because they will not leave you alone until you fulfill them. They always come with strong emotions. It's like a high mountain, you have to climb it and if you do not, you will perish. You will be like Esau who sold his birthright for a bowl of red beans. We must be able to distinguish the devil's voice and the mystery of it is that these voices are within *us*. We must be able to tell when certain inner voices are of God and when they are not. Certain inner voices may come in a positive way, but the result can be very catastrophic for your spiritual life. That is why you must be spiritually awake to be able to fight the battle (Eph. 6:11-18). You cannot go to war without arming yourself. If you don't, then the enemies will destroy you. That is why many Christians today don't go anywhere, spiritually speaking, because they are looking for an outside being as their enemy when the real enemy is destroying their life without them realizing it.

We know that there are unclean spirits out there, but if we are truly in God, they have no power over us. The only enemy that has power over us, is our own desire. It's our own lusts and carnal minds that we must watch over carefully and diligently. That is why Jesus said, "whosoever want to save his life, shall lose it, but whosoever would lose it for my name shall have it again." Life here is referring to the former life we had before conversion.

How to Become a Strong Leader of the Church

A leader must be strong in his character and sober in his attitudes. You cannot lead anything if you are a weak person. You cannot bring any change in people's lives if you are on the same level with them. A Leader must be morally and spiritually higher than the people, and he must bring them up to a higher dimension. As the people are growing, you too must grow. If not, then the people will reach your spiritual level, and you will no longer be able to lead them. When you are a leader, you must be a humble person, strong in your character and very meek in your spirit.

You must not be a proud person. A proud person cannot lead anything with true success. Somehow it will fail. This is because God hates proud people. Humility will help shape your character. Solomon said in the Book of Proverbs that the way up is down. Jesus said if a man does not become as a little child, he cannot become a productive leader in his kingdom.

A leader should not be a timid person. As a leader, you have been called to help the captives to become free, help the blind to able to see under your leadership and help the dead to be resurrected by the power of the word of God. To be able to do that, you must be able to speak without fear or intimidation. You word must be clear and very sharp. You must be able to convince and change the hearts of those listening to you. Then they will trust you and have great respect for you. If you are a timid person, you cannot achieve that at all. You must be able to overcome any intimidation but not with a bitter and hostile attitude. You should do it with compassion, tenderness, kindness and with a meek spirit and at the same time, be ready to exercise your authority to bring anyone who questions your integrity under submission.

A true leader leads without struggles. On the other hand, a bad leader always leads with all kinds of problems and unrest in his leadership. A leader should be able to bring peace and stability among the people. People are like the waves of the sea.

The only way to bring them to peace is to become a corrective force, which constantly corrects them until they get the picture.

To be a great and successful leader, you must be a great communicator. The only way you can successfully lead a people is to know the people who you are leading. To do that is to develop strong communication skills between yourself and the people. A true leader seeks to know the heart of every single individual under his leadership. Take note that if you are called to be the doctor of a group of people, you must first know their problems. Then you can give them medicine. If you don't do it this way, then you will be like a doctor who wants to heal people without knowing what kinds of sickness they are suffering from. Healing can come only if you know specifically what kind of disease you are dealing with. The same goes for people; you must get to know them to know their problems. You must be someone who has been called by God and who is equipped by God to do the job. If not and you try to do it on your own, you will fail.

To be a leader of a people, you must learn to listen to them, because you may find among them, a strong person who can help you lead stronger and more peacefully. Such a person knows the needs and the hearts of everyone because he has been there. You should never think you have it all and no one else is like you. You should not be a narrow-minded person. Instead, you should be an open-minded person. You should always be open to suggestion. Dealing with people is one of the most complex things you could ever have to deal with, because most of the time people hide their true motives.

The only way you can know their true motives is to become their friend and build a level of trust between them and you. Then they will begin to love you and trust you.

To gain people's trust is not an easy thing. It takes a lot of work and effort to do that. Leaders should not have the attitude of dominating the people, but an attitude to help them with their natural and spiritual needs. Take note that we are not called to be dictators, but to be builders in God's kingdom. A leader must be willing to share his authority and power with others, because you cannot achieve such great work alone. There can never be success without the sharing of power.

You must also be very wise and careful when it comes to selecting people to help you in your administration. Be aware that people with a goat-like nature cannot bear responsibilities! They will cause problems and division in your administration because they will not obey you. Their nature is to rebel against anything good. They will raise the people against you and overthrow you. That is the reason why, when it comes to selecting people to help you rule, you must be very careful. It is so easy to detect goat-like people. The way to do it is to humiliate them in public to see their reaction. Goat-like people don't like to be humiliated. They will curse you and run away. They are very proud, always protecting their personalities, and they are very protective for their names and their prestige. A humble person should be the one to select because he has an obedient spirit. They are the ones who will help you lead with peace and stability. They will not raise the people against you. They will obey your commands.

The Last Days

The Bible says, in 1 Thess. 5:1-8, "when men claim peace and safety a sudden destruction will come to destroy them." This verse clearly describes what will take place in these last days and how the world will come to an end. Almost every two thousand years God brings his judgment on the world. However, he always gives enough time for the righteous to escape the terrible events of his great judgment days. He always gives a chance to a group of people to separate themselves from the rest of the world. When God was ready to bring an end to the first world, he called Noah and his family to separate them from the rest of that wicked world and gave them a chance to escape the great flood (Gen. 6:8-21). When God was going to bring an end to the Jewish world, he had first established a judgment seat to separate the righteous from the unrighteous, and in A.D. 70 his great judgment day came and consumed all the rebels.

So it will be in our day. God will bring an end to this world! (Matt. 24:35) Heaven and earth is referring to the religious and civil power of this age (Matt. 3:12). Wheat symbolizes the true Christians and the chaff a figure of the civil and the religious power. Men are inventing many great things, believing that they are making provisions for the future, but the future is always in God's hand, not men. Just as Nimrod had built the Tower of Babel, believing that in it he would find safety for his people and himself, God brought confusion among them and they were not able to continue their foolish work because it did not please God. It was a movement of iniquity in the eyes of God. Men are trying to build space stations to be able to escape the great and terrible events of this age. We know that God is able to cast them down and confuse them from their evil works. It is easy to do things, but what is the motive behind it?

Facing the Great Giant

The Bible tells us, in Eph. 6:11, "put on the whole armor of God, that ye may be able to stand against the wiles of the devil. For we wrestle not against flesh and blood but against principalities, against power, against the rulers of the darkness of this world, against spiritual wickedness in high places." Who is our true enemy today? Many are looking for a being named Satan. They think that there is a force that causes them to fall into sin and do many evil things. Eph. 2:1-4 mentions the Prince of the Power of the Air. Verse 2 says that it's a "spirit that now worketh in the children of disobedience." He says that it's a spirit that is in us. That spirit is the spirit of the flesh. That is the great giant we have to fight against. Many great men of God bow down on bended knees before this giant. The reason is because they don't really know their true enemy.

The same way that David had to face the great Goliath is the way that we, as Christians following in Christ's footsteps, have to face the great temptations of the flesh. The only way that David destroyed the giant was to rely on God to help him do it. He could not rely on himself and expect to kill the giant. First of all, he was a little boy with no fighting skills, and second, the giant was well armed, highly skilled, and well trained. So it required a higher force to help David kill the giant. Goliath knew that David was just a little boy who wanted to die. David knew that he was not alone. He knew that God was with him. So it is with us. We must know that God is with us before entering the field of battle with a well skilled giant. We are not speaking about a natural giant here. That is why Paul mentioned that our spiritual warfare is not against flesh and blood but against spirits in high places. What he meant when he says wicked spirits in high places was our desires. High levels of imagination pushed by our emotions could cause us to do things that are contrary to the law of God. That is what we must watch with a very high interest things that the carnal mind wants that you cannot give in to. That's when you come to the way where you cannot fulfill your lust anymore, where you are denying your wants. You are stabbing the great giant, causing him to die every day. As I have said before, the great giant is not a literal giant like Goliath. It's a spiritual giant, the great giant of the flesh, and he is more powerful and more destructive then the physical giant.

We must reach a position where we have full control over our desires. Why have so many great men of God bent their knees before the flesh? It's because they don't really know the depths of it, so they take it lightly. That is how it destroys so many great men who started out very good with God. That is why it's so important not to hide your weaknesses. When someone has a weakness in his or her life and they don't take it seriously, it could destroy their lives later on. The flesh is not something we should play with. It's something that we must expose to death daily. We must not fulfill its lust and its excess demands (Gal. 5:16-21).

There are three main ways we can compromise with the flesh. The first is by woman, the second is money, and the third is power. These areas are the main ways the devil has to trap many great men of God and many saints. When you love women too much, you will find a secret way to get women, thinking that no one will know because it's a secret. And when you are there, you will need money to please these women. That is where you dig your own hole, and you will later fall into it. God is omnipresent, omnipotent and omniscient. We cannot hide ourselves before him. That is why we must be honest with ourselves, knowing that God is the one who will reward us for our good behavior and conduct in the church.
Knowing also that we are not here permanently but that we are here just to fulfill the will of God, according to his purpose for our lives, and that we will not compromise that for anything of this world.

Who are the True Israelites?

The Bible says in Rom. 2:29, "but he is a Jew, which is one inwardly; and circumcision is that of the heart in the spirit and not in the letter; whose praise is not of men but of God." Jesus told the Jews that He was the way, the truth, and life, no one could or would go to God but by him. This is a radical statement. This meant that the natural Jews no longer had the special privileges they used to have under the law, since the first covenant was removed and a second one had been established (Heb. 8:7). Heb. 8:10 says that the true covenant that God made was the covenant where he gave us his spirit. He says that this is a different covenant, not like the one he had with the Jews. The Bible says, in John 1, "to them that believe, he gave power to become the sons of God." I believe that the true Christians, are the spiritual Jews since the word Jew means, call of God. We are the true Jews because we were called by God to become a holy nation, a spiritual nation.

The special privileges the Israelites had no longer existed, because they must come to Jesus to find salvation for their souls. In 1 John 4:20-24, we read how Jesus had a deep conversation with the Samaritan woman where she told Jesus that her fathers had worshipped on top of a certain mountain. Jesus' answer to her was very surprising. Jesus told her that "the time has come, where it shall be neither on this mountain, nor in Jerusalem, ye shall worship the Father. The hour is come where the true worshippers shall worship the Father in truth and in spirit. And he said God is a spirit, those who worship him must worship in spirit and in truth." Jesus wanted to show the Samaritan woman that they no longer had that special privilege, and they must be spiritual to be able to worship God, that they were not spiritual, they were carnal. That was the main reason they were not able to maintain a high spiritual standard that would please God. They knew they had a special birthright and that once they were born in Israel they automatically became special people before God. So they began to lose respect for God, taking his word lightly, until God said it was enough and sent His judgment on the system and established another covenant.

It is not whether or not you were born in Israel that makes you more important, but your spiritual values, virtues and qualities, especially when you received the baptism of the Holy Ghost, because that is when you become the sons of God! The kingdom of God is no longer in Israel, but the kingdom of God on the earth today is under the name of the church. It's a church where the Holy Spirit has full access to the spirit, soul and body of the saints. The Holy Spirit is the essence of God. Once you receive it, you become a living soul. That is why it's no longer a place, but it's a spiritual birth that counts before God today. The Jews must come to Jesus, just as we Gentiles do, to have peace with God. If they choose not to do this, then they will never see salvation for their souls.

The GodHead

The God Head is the basis of the power and the authority of God (Rom 1:2) (Coloss. 2:2-10). Jesus Christ, the Son of God, had revealed all the mysteries of God, especially the mystery of godliness. As Jesus spoke to the great multitude in the parable, so is the mysteries of God for the human race.

In Jesus dwells all the power of divinity (Coloss. 1:19). God put all the fullness of his power in Jesus (1 Tim 3:16-17). So there is a great mystery in the GodHead that is very difficult to understand without God himself revealing it to you (1 Cor. 5:6). Jesus was conceived by the Holy Ghost, by this we know that God is Jesus' father. We want to know where some religions find the three gods that they are preaching about. The Holy Ghost is not a person! The Holy Ghost is a spirit, the spirit of a person. So if the Holy Ghost is not a person, this means that there are only two in the God Head. God the Father is the absolute and the original authority, established from everlasting to everlasting. This God the Father has no other authority above him. He is the only true, eternal God, who has no beginning or end (1 Tim. 2:5). Jesus is the second authority in the GodHeadG because in 1 Tim. 1:15-17 it says, "who is the image of the invisible God, the first born of every creature. For he created all things, visible and invisible, whether there are thrones or dominions or principalities or powers: all things were created by Him and for Him: after God the Father, Jesus is the second authority in Heaven and over the church."

God the Father is all in all. He is the original source of all things. Jesus had his authority from him directly and he reported only to God the Father. That is why he is sitting at his right hand in Heaven.

1 Cor. 8:6 says that there is only one God, and from him come all things and we have one Savior and by him are all things. The very important point mentioned here is that there is only one God. Then it says that everything is of God, by Jesus Christ. 1 Tim. 2:5 says that there's only one God and one mediator between God and men, and that mediator is Christ

Jesus. There is only one mediator working for the human race, he is Jesus (John 10:33). The Jews answered him saying, "for a good work we stone thee not; but for blasphemy; and because that thou being a man makest thyself God." Jesus answered them, in verse 34-38, "is it not written in your law, I said ye are gods? If he called them gods, unto whom the word of God came, and the scripture cannot be broken. Say ye of him whom the Father had sanctified and sent into the world, thou blasphemes; because I said, I am the Son of God? If I do not the works of my Father, believe me not. But if I do though ye that believe me not, believe that the Father is in me and I in him.

Jesus wanted the Jewish people to become one with God as he is one with God but they categorically refused to accept Jesus as their savior. John 17:20-24 says that the glory that Jesus had came from God. Another important point to mention here is that Jesus said the Father loves him before the foundation of the world. This means that Jesus existed before he was conceived by Mary (John 17:5) (Rev 3:14). Jesus was the very first being that God created (Coloss. 1:15-27). This shows us that Jesus was the image of the invisible God (Heb. 1:1-2). This shows us that God had appointed Jesus as the heir of all things and all things were created by him (John 1:3). This shows us that God created Jesus and Jesus created all things (1 Cor. 15:24-28). This shows us that at the end of time, Jesus will return all the power and authority to God because that is from whom he had received it (Dan. 7:13). There will be a day that Jesus will rule the whole world by through the church (1 Peter 3:22) (Rev. 2:26).

So as we dwell in Jesus, we will receive the power to become rulers of this world (Psalms 45:7-8). In this scripture we look at Jesus as our God, but note that Jesus himself is a God but God the Father is the original authority who has no beginning or end. He is the everlasting God, all in all. There is no place in the Bible where we can clearly see three Gods, as they preach in the religious world. As I said in previous chapters, the Holy Ghost is not a person but the spirit of a person. The Holy Ghost is the essence of God. It is the creative power of God, not a person. Jesus is an identity. So is God the Father. He is also an identity, but the Holy Spirit does not have an identity. Nowhere can we prove that in the Bible.

The Three Phases of Salvation

In the religious world, preachers sermonize about an eternal security. They tell the people once they come to Christ and repent, they are eternally secure. If they die the next day, they will go to Heaven. In the Body of Christ we preach the three phases of salvation. The first phase is "I am saved"; the second phase is "I am on my way to be saved," and the third phase is "I shall be saved."

The first phase deals with our past sins. When someone comes to Christ, accepts him as Lord and Savior of their lives and properly receives water baptism, that takes care of all their past sins. When God baptizes you with the Holy Spirit with the evidence of speaking in other tongues, you become white as snow. All your past sins are now washed away. You become a new creature in Christ (John 3:3, 5-6). Take note that after these great steps, you are only saved from the world. That does not mean that you have made it. There are still two other great processes to go through. Just like the children of Israel had left Egypt but Egypt never left them, it took God forty years to take Egypt out of them. So when you leave the world, that doesn't mean that the world leaves you. When you come to Christ and confess with your mouth that Jesus is Lord and recognize that you are a sinner, that takes care of all your sins. You are not yet ready to go to Heaven! There must be a preparation in your life first, and sometimes it takes a whole lifetime. Heaven is a reward, not a gift. The first phase of the salvation is indeed a gift, but it's only the first phase. It's free to come to Christ and to make peace with God.

The second and third phases require heavy work. When a preacher teaches someone that when they are converted he or she is saved forever, that is wrong. It's true that you are saved but not to go to Heaven. You are saved from the world.

Now it's up to you to keep yourself out of the world. The fact is that your sins are now forgiven, and you must keep yourself clean. If after all that you decide to go back and get yourself dirty again, believing that Jesus' grace will clean you again, you are wrong. It depends on the severity of your sin. God never forgives intentional sins. When you come to Christ, you are just a baby. God cannot punish you for wrongdoing, the same way that you would not severely punish your own baby for wrongdoing, because the baby is not fully aware of what he or she is doing. However, as the child begins to grow, you must then begin to correct and punish the child. So it is with God. That is how he treats us as we come to him as our original and true Father. He will not destroy us for our wrongdoing, but he will correct us until we learn to walk in the straight way.

What we must watch the most are intentional sins. After being cleaned, you must keep a clean record, because after someone has received the baptism of the Holy Ghost, his or her name is now written in the Book of Life, which is the memory of God. Everything that you do is recorded, and that is how you will be judged worthy or unworthy of eternal life.

The second phase of salvation deals with the Adamic nature. Remember that I told you when the Israelites left Egypt, Egypt did not leave them. It took God forty years to take Egypt out of them. After they were finally ready to possess the land, they had to face the nations that lived on the land and had to fight to possess the land. It is the same way for brothers and sisters in Christ. When we come to Christ, we have a sinful nature in us that we cannot take to Heaven.

That is why God instituted the church, to prepare us, to clean us with the water of the word. So we could grow to become fully mature adults and not remain children all our lives. It also takes the baptism of the Holy Ghost to give us power over this sinful nature, because it's so strong and powerful that we alone would not be able to overcome such a nature. It takes God to help us do it. When we enter into this phase we are fighting to become the sons and daughters of God, because now we are facing the enemy and the enemy is within ourselves (John 1:12). The word *becoming* in John 1:12, insinuates a long process, and it could take a whole lifetime.

The second phase is mainly dealing with the fact that the Adamic nature must be put to death for us to become strong adults in God. We cannot remain children and expect to be in the second phase of our salvation. After the Holy Ghost baptizes us, it is the arrangement and preparation we make in our lives that really put us into the second phase. These preparations will allow us to become spiritual. Without spirituality we cannot save our souls from death (1 Peter 2:3-5). We must do our best to draw near to God to become a part of his spiritual house today. How can we draw ourselves near to God? We do that by doing our best in practicing personal holiness and by denying the flesh of all its wants. Then we will begin to grow spiritually. The second phase is the dying process and also a resurrecting process. "And be renewed in the spirit of your mind and that ye put on the new man, which after God is created in righteousness and true holiness (Coloss. 2:20-21) (Eph. 4:23-24). "Speaking the truth in love, may grow up into him in all things, which is the head of Christ" (Eph. 4:15). The same way the Israelites had to destroy all the enemies in the land to possess the land, it's the same way that we Christians must destroy all the deed of the flesh in our lives to possess our souls.

The Third Phase of Salvation

The third phase is God's supernatural action to purify our souls. That is when we must be very careful, because this phase is the one in which we must prove ourselves to God as pure gold. God will begin to test our faith to prove to him who we really are. It is the kind of action that God takes to begin a purification process in our lives. In it we prove ourselves either worthy or unworthy of eternal life. That process is the baptism of fire. It is the process in which we could truly say, "I shall be saved." It is the phase that Paul the Apostle reached when he said, "I have fought the good fight, I have finished my course, I have kept the faith: a crown of righteousness, which the Lord, the righteous judge shall give me at that day: and not to me only but unto all them also that love his appearing." God had taken Paul through some serious purification process before he could say that he had reached the mark and that a crown of righteousness was reserved for him. Before Paul could say that, he went through many great tribulations, and through these things, God had purified his soul of all the great sins he had committed in the past. It is going to be the same for you and me. God will take us through some purification process to purify our souls. It's little by little that God sends his fire upon us because he knows that we could not bear it all at once. It would consume us. The key point here is to differentiate between the fire that God sent to us to help us get in the right way and the fire that we created ourselves. The fire that we create ourselves will not help us purify our souls. Only God's fire can purify us. When we say fire, we don't mean a natural fire, we mean trials and tribulations that we have to face for the cause of the gospel. However, it has to be for the cause of the gospel. If we do evil things that cause us trouble, then we have no profit in them.

Sabbath

What is the true definition of the word Sabbath? What was the purpose of it? Why had God asked the children of Israel to practice Sabbath? We find in Genesis 2:2-3 that on the seventh day the Lord rested from his work, and he had blessed the seventh day. First of all, we need to know what the seventh day is. Was it describing a period of time, perhaps years, in which the Lord had taken to complete natural creation? And how many years do each day represent?

We know that the word Sabbath means rest. If God had rested from his works, what is our work today as Christians? Is it also part of our duty to rest from our works one day? Or did God really only mean for us to rest our physical bodies every Saturday? We need to know that God had also made a promise to all his faithful servants to enter his rest. Remember that he said to the children of Israel that they will not enter in his rest. So if it were only the physical rest, then God would not promise another rest. We need to differentiate between the literal resting that God gave to the children of Israel, and the rest of God (Heb. 4:1).

The reasons that God commanded the whole nation to practice natural Sabbath were; first because it was a figure of the spiritual Sabbath; and second because they were all slaves, and they had worked seven days a week. So it was necessary for them to have a day of rest just to commemorate and normalize their lives.

Notice that we are no longer under the law of Moses but under the law of the spirit of life which is in Christ Jesus. As it is said in Heb. 10:1, "For the law of Moses had a shadow of good things to come, and not the very image of the thing.

Never with those sacrifices which they offered year by year continually make comers'there unto perfect. For then would they not have cease to be offered because the worshippers once purged should have had no more conscience of sins." Verse 3 says, "but in those sacrifices there is a remembrance again made of sins every year. For it is not possible that the blood of bulls and goats should take away sins." "If therefore perfection were by the Leviticus priesthood, (for under it the people received the law) what further need was there that another priest should rise after the order of Mel-chise-dec, and not be called after the order of Aaron, for the priesthood being changed there is made of necessity a change also of the law," (Herb.7:11). Jesus said, in Matt. 11:28, "come unto me all ye that labor and are heavy laden, and I will give you rest." What kind of rest was it that Jesus promised to everyone who came to Him? In the twenty-ninth verse he says rest for your souls. He never said to rest for your bodies, but for your souls. How can someone find rest for his soul in Jesus? First we need to know that the Holy Ghost's baptism is the beginning of our rests in God, but we also need to understand that there's a long process to it. You must carefully work with your salvation to enter into the rest of God.

We have nothing against people or cults that want to rest for a day or two during the week, but they need to understand that it's not a law anymore. Resting for a day has nothing to do with the salvation of your soul. Notice that God made no provision for our bodies, but he did make provisions for our souls. That's what is important for God. So if observance of natural days can give us rest for our souls, then it would not be important for Jesus to come and die for our redemption.

Preachers even mention in their sermons that if someone is not practicing the natural Sabbath, they will not go to Heaven (Heb. 8:7). Paul says that if the first covenant had been faultless, then no place should have been sought for a second one.

So if the first covenant was abolished, then why do we have to observe the Sabbath, since Sabbath was one of the ordinances of the old covenant? When something is abolished it means it no longer exists. Then why do we have to practice it? He did not say that the first covenant was partially abolished. We know that because there is another one that was established. That is how we know. Some people even say that it's only the ceremonial part of it but the Law still exists. That's not so. The whole 600 ordinances were completely abolished because Jesus had established another one. We have to ask ourselves why most of Jesus' miracles always happened on the Sabbath day. It was because Jesus wanted to show the Jewish religious world the changing of the law, but anytime he performed a miracle on the Sabbath day they were very furious and they wanted to kill him.

The man with the withered hand was the next healing episode reported by all three synopses, (Matt.12:9-21) (Mark 3:1-6). These two chapters show to us how Jesus begins his Sabbath reforms. They brought the man with the withered hand to him. They brought the man just to see if Jesus would dare to heal him on the Sabbath day, in order to find a way to accuse him of violating the law (Mark 3:2) (Matt.12: 9-11). They asked Jesus if it's lawful to heal on the Sabbath days. Jesus asked them, "what man should there be among you that shall have one sheep, and if it fall into a pit on the Sabbath day will he not lay hold on it, and lift it out. How much then is a man better than a sheep.

Wherefore it is lawful to do well on the Sabbath days. The real Sabbath is the spiritual one but we must qualify ourselves to enter into the spiritual Sabbath of God."

The fact is that God is resting from the work of natural creation, but he is not retired from the spiritual work. God still rules the universe. He is the supreme chief above all! We say that the Sabbath is three-dimensional: it commemorated the past, present and future deliverance. The weekly relief from the hardships of natural work cannot, in any shape or form, have anything to do with the spiritual rest that God promised to his faithful servants. The rest that God had promised is only for those who had worked hard to prove themselves worthy to Him. They will have the privilege of entering into the rest of God. It's a reward for those who worked, so if someone did not work, they would not have the privilege to enter into the rest of God. God had worked, so he has rested from his works.

Heb. 8:8 says, "for finding fault with them he said behold, the day is come said the Lord when I will make a new covenant with the house of Israel and with the house of Judah! Not according to the covenant that I made with their fathers when I took them by the hand to lead them out of the land of Egypt because they had not continued in my covenant, and I regarded them not, said the Lord." When someone decides to practice the natural Sabbath, he or she must practice the whole Law of Moses, without skipping even one. We know that can be very difficult to do, especially in this time that we are living. That is why Jesus had come to give us power (the Holy Ghost), so we could become true sons and daughters of God. The law of the spirit of life in Christ asks us to live above the law of Moses. The law was good but it cannot bring any soul into perfection.

The law of the spirit of life in Christ asks us to purge ourselves to maintain a high level of personal holiness and to love our brothers and sisters in Christ. The Blood of Jesus purified our past sins, and the Holy Ghost gives life to our souls and helps us to maintain a high moral standard. Things that we could not do under the law of Moses. So if Jesus had taken away the burden of the law, He makes it possible for us to come before God as sons and daughters. I don't see why people want to go back to a law that had been replaced by a better one; the law of the spirit of life in Jesus Christ. It's a great mystery to see people who want to practice the Sabbath, that are not even born of spirit. They remain natural, and nothing has changed. They think that by observing one day in the week is sufficient for them to go to Heaven. John 3:6 says, "that which is born of flesh is flesh; and that which is born of spirit is spirit." Rom.10:4 says that "Jesus is the end of the law for the righteousness to everyone who believe". I don't understand why some preachers want to justify their doctrines, ignoring what is written in the New Testament books. Paul, one of the greatest Apostles who ever lived, says that Jesus Christ's coming on the earth was the end of the law of Moses. If something is ended this means it no longer exists. If it does not exist anymore, why would some people want to still practice the law. Paul says the law was not made for religious people or Christians, but that it was made for the ungodly, the wicked, the adulteress' and the fornicators. When we accepted becoming a part of the family of God on the earth, we could not make ourselves slaves of the law anymore. For the precious blood of our Lord and savior Jesus Christ cleaned us from all that is unclean, and we became pure and white like snow. We became sons and daughters of God, to be reconciled by the principal angel of God. However, they had their eyes on the law, ignoring the spiritual law of everlasting life provided under the new covenant through his son, Jesus Christ. Jesus came with the spiritual law. For in it is the secret of the everlasting life. We know that under the law of Moses the spirit of God was not fully released to the human race. After the fall of Adam and Eve, God said that men are nothing more than flesh, and his spirit shall not always dwell in them. The children of Israel did not find rest in the law, as I had said before because the law was only the shadow of things to come. In it were all the shadows and types of all things to come (spiritual things). The hearts of the children of Israel were so wicked that it was necessary for them to have a law to guide them into the righteousness of God. When they left Egypt they took with them all the idolatries and the uncleanness of Egypt. Remember that they were born in Egypt, so they were practically Egyptians born from the Hebrews.

The Egyptians were idolaters. They worshipped many false gods, and God hates idolaters. That was why most of them had perished in the desert. In their imaginations they thought that the land of Canaan was going to be a rest for them, because they did not understand that the kind of rest that God had promised them was a spiritual rest. It's true that the land of Canaan was a symbol of the spiritual rest, but it was not the exact thing. Remember, they had to fight first to possess the land. So the land of Canaan is a symbol of our souls!

The same way they had to fight with the wicked and ungodly people who were on the land in order to possess the land, so do we. We must fight with wicked and unclean spirits that live in our lives in order to possess our souls. If we don't do that, those spirits will destroy us.

The children of Israel had compromised with the people, so they became an everlasting torment for them up until now, because they disobeyed the law of God. So the land of Canaan was not the rest, because it says in the book of Hebrews (Heb. 4:8) that Joshua did not give them the rest! Jesus came to give the rest to all of those who came to Him to have peace with God.

All the true Christians could one day enter into the peace of God, but we must work very hard for it. I am sure that all the apostles of Christ entered into God's peace. Take note that they had first worked hard and gave their lives for the cause of the gospel. So God rewarded them with eternal life, which is the true rest of God.

Many people think that rest comes after they die when they go straight to Heaven, but rest is an angelical body. In it dwells immortality. If you are qualified to receive it, then your soul could live in it forever. That is the true rest. God is a great liberator.

This call to remember the great deliverance that God had provided to the Israelites was a great experience for them. Still, all of them were not free from the idols of Egypt. They had remained slaves even though they were not physically living in Egypt. The spirits of Egypt kept them in slavery until they died. Most of them fell in the wilderness, and their flesh had rotted. Hell had opened its mouth and swallowed them, and they were perished forever.

In this present dispensation, God is now calling his people out of a religious system by millions. Those who obey him will enter his rest! But all of those who harden their hearts will remain there and will face his judgment day.

The Jewish religious world had to face the judgment day of the Lord in A.D. 70, and most of them perished. They missed God's salvation, which was offered by Jesus! It will be the same at the end of this age. Many will miss the Sabbath of the Lord because they are in complete ignorance. They do not really understand God's plan for the human race. God will redeem those who were seeking Him diligently and wisely.

We don't want to become like the foolish virgins who did not have enough oil in their lamp, thereby missing the great day of the Lord. While we have the opportunity to buy oil to put in our lamps, we must take it. Oil in the Bible is a symbol, which means the understanding of the word of God.

People must know that a lowly man or woman, who serves God, is better than a proud man or woman in the world! God calls us to be humble. If we think we already know everything about God, then we miss it because God is a God who deals in mysteries.

There's nothing simple in God, so all of those who seem to be wise and prudent get trapped in their own nests.

That's exactly what had happened to the Pharisees and the Sadducees in the time of Jesus. They thought that they were all wise and prudent. They needed no one else to tell them about God, because they already knew everything about God.

People with such misconceptions always miss what God is doing. Yet, if we humble ourselves and become like children, then God will help us and allow us to understand his plan. Nevertheless, those who pretend to be wise and self-righteous will never see or understand the plan of God. Christians should be open-minded.

That doesn't mean that we should swallow anything we hear, but any true Christian who has received the true Holy Spirit of God has the potential to know the truth when they hear it, because they have in them the essence of God. The spirit of God will never leave them in ignorance of the things of God, but proud people always miss what God is doing because God hates proud people (Prov. 6:17).

Whatever God is doing in every age or time period, He always reveals it to the humble people! Because there are two types of people in the human race, the righteous and the unrighteous, God will never reveal his plan to those who are predestined to perish not because it's His plan for them to perish, but because it's not in their nature to obey. People from the unrighteous live like goats! They have a rebellious nature. They would rather die then obey. That is their nature. People from the righteous line are like lambs! They love the truth. When they hear the truth of the word of God, they know it and they will die for the truth. People with goat natures cannot enter the rest of God! It's impossible.

People should never close their minds to learning something new. Because God deals in mystery, no one really has it all! But God is gradually revealing His plan to a group of holy men in this present age. Narrow-minded people will miss what God is about to do in this age because they are not humble. God never reveals his plan at once! That's the reason why men cannot comprehend God's mysteries. Only Jesus, Moses and the twelve apostles understood God in a way that no other human can. They were called by God and had received the special touch of the Holy Spirit without measure. Paul the apostle had even experienced the taste of the third Heaven while he was in his flesh.

This is something that any other human being had ever experienced before, not even the other eleven apostles. The third Heaven is the holiest of all, the very presence of God, and the place of God's throne.

Since the fall of the early church, men invented many things. They interpreted the Bible literally, and the Bible is not a literal book! It is true that God had at one time told the Israelites to practice literal Sabbath, but there is a spiritual Sabbath also. The problem is that people only see the natural Sabbath. They close their minds to learning about the spiritual Sabbath, which is the real Sabbath.

Whenever God tells men to do something literal, there's always a spiritual event that the natural one is foreshadowing. The spiritual one is the one that always reveals God's perfect will. There was a natural Adam first, but Jesus is the spiritual Adam! There was a natural covenant, there is a spiritual covenant. There was a natural nation of Israel and there's also a spiritual nation of Israel.

Men are so blind they cannot see these things. They are always criticizing what they cannot understand. Every body is defending what they believe to be true and they stick to it. As I said before, that's what happened to the Pharisees and the Sadducees.

They thought that they had God, and no one else knew more about God. They thought that everyone should come to them, so they could teach them but the reality was that they did not know anything about God. They thought they knew, but they were all ignorant. We know that God is a God of mercy, a God of principle, a holy God who will not forgive intentional sins. That's why it was a surprise to them when God judged them in A.D. 70 They had received the wrath of God in all its fullness. Only those who had obeyed Jesus' message escaped.

It's going to be the same for the rebels of our time. God will judge these false religious systems the same way! They will drink in the cup of wrath of God, and they will say Lord, we have done many miracles in your name. We have prophesied in your name. Jesus will rebuke them saying that he did not know them (Matt 7:22-23). Jesus said that not everybody who calls him Lord would enter Heaven (Matt 7:21). That's why we should be like the wise man who had built his house on the rock. The Bible says that when a strong wind came and his house stood, it was because it was built on the rock, unlike the foolish man who had built his house on sand. When strong wind comes, great will be the destruction of his house because it had been built on sand. Today everyone is building their houses, and every single one of them claims that they are building for God. Still there will be a day where God himself shall test all of them. If they stand after the test, they will be rewarded, but if their house collapses, they will perish (1 Cor. 3:12-14).

Everyone who had preached false doctrines to God's people would be judged much more severely than the ungodly because they kept God's people in ignorance, which caused them to miss God's salvation. When Jesus was here, he did not preach traditions to the people! He preached only the truth to them, and he had saved them with the truth, not with traditions. Jesus was not spiritually blind; that's why he was able to lead the blind. Jesus says if a blind man is leading other blind people, they shall all fall in a ditch!

He also says your eyes are the lights of the body. If your eyes are not in good shape, the whole body will be in darkness. Eyes in the Bible, is a symbol of leadership in the church.

If a pastor is teaching false doctrines, he will lead you directly into a deep hole. If you become a member in a religious system or cult, don't just close your eyes and accept everything they teach you. You must be obedient to your pastor and the system you belong to, but at the same time you must let your five spiritual senses fully develop. If you feel something is not going right don't just accept it. Ask questions and pray to God to reveal the truth. I am sure that God will show you, even in a dream. Jesus said those who ask shall receive. This is a promise! So if we ask with a sincere heart, God will answer our prayers.

God will not answer fanatics, but he will answer true Christians who are seeking God with a sincere heart. The saints of the church today have become spiritually blind because lack a sincere heart and have become too fanatical. They are not seeking God in order to change themselves, they just want to be religious. Do you see how you can be religious and never become a Christian? Christians are those who follow the lamb wherever He goes. How do you follow the lamb wherever he goes? In Isaiah we see a picture of it. The prophet saw a wheel in the middle of another wheel and two wings attached into them. The middle wheel had eyes all around and they are moving together. This reveals the everlasting plan of God throughout the ages. Remember that an eye *in the Bible is* a symbol of ministers, and note that the wheels were moving.

The wheels symbolized the plan of God throughout eternity. This means that the plan of God is moving, and the eyes are able to see the plan of God for the human race.

In every age or dispensation, God always has a group of ministers who know His plan, and it's only those who remain attached with the wheels.

Jesus says, in John 15:1-7, "I am the true vine and my father is the husband man. If a branch remains attached in me, he will bear good fruit. If he does not remain attached to the main vine, he will be cut-off, ready to be burned in fire". Not all of the pastors out there are in the perfect will of God! Jesus says that you will know them by their fruits.

The Chariot of God

Many members of the lathering church will lose out when the time comes to pass where God begins to purify His church of all its unclean deeds! Many will miss the chariot of God (2 King 2:11). Some of those so-called Christians of our time will miss that great day, and some will regret that they didn't take it seriously to go all the way with God. Brothers and sisters, we have a chance to enter into eternity. The only way we can possibly make it, is to hold tight to the chariot of God. We cannot go all the way with God if we don't have a clear vision and the determination to hold tight to the end. We need to have the conviction not to look back. In Rom. 2:7-8 Paul says, "to them who by patient continuance in well doing seek for glory and honor and immortality, eternal life: but unto them that are contentious, and do not obey the truth but obey unrighteousness, indignation and wrath."

The chariot of God is a picture of the church under the dispensation of grace. "And it came to pass, as they still went on, and talked, that behold, there appeared a chariot of fire, and horses of fire, and parted them both asunder; and Elijah went up" (2 King 2:11). The chariot of fire that Elisha saw was a sign of the church in our times because going to Heaven is not in this manna any more. It had happened only for Elisha in the manna. The only way people can possibly go to Heaven is by the church of God.

The church has stopped moving since the death of the twelve apostles. There will be a glorious church in our time too, but only those who sanctified themselves will be able to become partakers of it. When the church returns to its glory, we will see the glorious fire of God surrounding the church! This is not literally speaking but spiritually. The chariot of God, which is the church, will take us into eternity. We have a destination. Our destination is to enter in the everlasting kingdom of God, and only those who dedicate their lives to God who will become partakers of it. When the chariot of God starts moving, as it was in the early times, many will lose out. Only a few will make it at the end and enter into eternity. Those who have the chance to enter into eternity will see the face of Jesus, spiritually speaking. They will be able to see the difference between man's rotten world and the world of God. Many wicked Christians will be resurrected to see the beauty of it, then die again forever (Rev. 20:4-8).

The Law of Sowing and Reaping

Paul says, "but this I say, he which soweth sparingly shall reap also sparingly. And he which soweth bountifully shall reap also bountifully" (2 Cor. 9:11). This is one of the most powerful laws and one of the best-hidden secrets that not everyone can understand. I would say that if everyone in the world or in the church truly understood the law of giving and reaping, every single individual would be blessed abundantly!

The greatest problem facing the church today is that Christians don't have enough faith in God when it comes to giving their money to the church. They always think that when they give, the pastor is the one who's getting rich. Some people are so selfish that they don't even want their pastors who are leading them to have anything from the money they give to the church. The Bible says that when you give you shall also reap. It's a law! We must know that whatever you sow in life you will indeed reap. Good or bad, it is a law.

There are four kinds of sowing. The first one is when a man has intercourse with a woman, and he sows his natural seed in the woman. Nine months later she will give birth to a baby. Everyone can see the fruit of his sowing. The second kind, is when someone takes a natural seed, and sows it in the ground and so that after a certain time the seed will spring up from the ground and produce a tree according to its kind. Third is the sowing of the word. Good or bad both will bring forth their fruits. When someone sows a negative word in another person's ears, his words will leave their fruits in that person's life. However, it will be a bad fruit. Words are the power of life and can also be the power of death. The good, productive and creative word of God will produce life when it is sown in someone's life. The negative and destructive words of an animal man will produce death in anyone's soul, even though he may know the truth of the word of God. Words have the power to create and the power to destroy! That is why we should not play with what comes out of our mouths because it may effect someone's life. The fourth kind of sowing is when you're sowing your money. A generous person always gives with joy and without murmuring.

Such a person can never become poor because he's always sowing his seed. Why do you think some people always have to give, while others are always lacking everything? They're always striving to survive. It is because the secret of prosperity is giving. To prosper in life you must give. Those who don't like to give never get blessed!

The Bible says that there are more blessings to give than to receive. Some people in the world know that secret, so they get rich and they have abundance. Why do you think that some great movie actors in Hollywood always donate millions of dollars every year? It's because they know the law of sowing and reaping. They know that the more they give, the more they will make. They sow their seed by faith. That's what God wants from us! He wants us to act by faith and he will bless us abundantly.

If people of the world know to act by faith, what about us Christians of the latering church? Shouldn't we know better? Christians of our days don't have enough faith to sow their seed, even in the kingdom of God of which they are members. We know that the kingdom of God is the best place to sow our seeds, because we know for sure that we will reap them abundantly. We all know that the best sowing is when you sow spiritual things in both the kingdom of God and in the outer world. When you sow spiritual things in people who are dying in this world of darkness, they come to the light with their eyes open, and they give their lives to God. It is a great blessing. You help gain a soul that was lost in the world. God takes note of that, and your reward will be great.

What about those who use their negative words to destroy the faith of those who are already in the Kingdom? Paul says in Gal. 6:7-9, "Be not deceived, God cannot be mocked, for whatsoever man soweth, he shall also reap. For he that soweth to his flesh shall reap of the flesh corruption; but he that soweth to the spirit shall reap of the spirit life everlasting." Chapter six of Galatians is clearly showing to us the law of sowing and reaping. When someone destroys the hope of everlasting life in a saint, your reward will be everlasting death. For some people, their job in the church is to become a judge. Judging things that they don't even understand, and that kind of attitude affects new converters in Christ.

We must know that there are seven dynamic ways of prosperity, and without these seven principles, no one can possibly prosper in anything. The first principle is giving. The second is faith in God. The third is positive thinking. The fourth is to write your goals on paper and refine them every once in a while. The fifth is your attitudes and perceptions. Six is to be positive about life itself. And seven is that your motives must be right.

Your thoughts are like internal regulators that determine whether you will succeed or fail. Anything you are doing in life is what your thoughts make it to be. So the key that can open any door for you in life is your thoughts. Thoughts and beliefs work together to produce a maximum effect. The most important point is your subconscious mind. Whatever you house in your subconscious mind will walk its way out into your natural and even your financial life. People must realize that they can become whatever they want to become in life, but there's a catch. You must house positive thoughts in your subconscious mind, and what you think is what you will eventually become. There's no doubt about it.

The fourth key, as I said, was to write your main goals on a piece of paper, and every week or so you should refine your goals. As you are doing this, you're planting the picture into your mind. And when the mind finally accepts it as a reality, your subconscious mind will begin to work to bring it into effect.

Your fifth key is your attitudes and perceptions. Your attitudes about life are the most important factor to succeed in life. Haven't you ever seen people who always have negative things to say about life? Often these people live miserably.

You must be in perfect harmony with life in order to succeed in life. If your perception is negative, you will reap the negative fruit of life. After awhile, for people who are like that, it will become a mental habit. They live a life of frustration and bitterness. Finally they remain where they are until they die. It's because negative thoughts always block any effort that they make to try to succeed.

The sixth key as I said, is to be positive in anything you are doing in life. Positive thinking produces maximum results. If you are trying to do something and believe you can succeed, you will. If you plan to do something that could change your whole life and you begin to have doubts about succeeding, you will fail. Don't let that little inner voice tell you negative things. Anytime it tries to, ignore it; believe you can succeed and you will.

The seventh way, if your motives are not right in everything you are doing in life, even though you may succeed, you will fail, after all because your mind is like a fertilized ground and your thoughts are like seeds.

Whatever seed you put in your mind will grow and will affect your life differently. That's why your motives must be right, because your inward thought is actually the power that governs your life. Both motives and motivations must be in harmony to succeed in life. In order words, if you want to succeed in life you can, and nothing can possibly stop you if you really put your mind into it and believe it. But if you want to succeed in life, just to be in competition with another person, then your motives are not right. You must be strongly motivated to succeed in life, and your motivation must be pushed by strong emotions to drive it into your subconscious mind.

Have you ever asked yourself what motivates some people to achieve such great success in life? They had strong enough motivations to make their goals a reality. Without motivations you cannot go anywhere in life. It is just like if you want to go somewhere naturally, you must be motivated to get in your car, start the engine and drive there. It's the same in life. Your motivations will help you start but remember, you must keep pressing until it becomes a reality.

The second key, concerning having faith. Paul says, in Heb. 11:1 that faith is the substance of things hoped for and the evidence of things not seen. Being without faith is like having a car but not having the gas to drive it anywhere. Paul says that faith is a substance of things you hoped for. It means that faith is the power. Anything you truly want in life you can get. Through faith you can cause it to become a reality. Now there are people who only have faith in themselves and not in God. There's nothing wrong when you have confidence in yourself. In fact you must have confidence in yourself to achieve success in life, but there's a danger in it! It's when you believe something, and it comes to pass and you begin boasting and thinking that it's by your own power and strength that you were able to achieve such a great wonder. God hates proud people! Never let your heart become proud when something good happens in your life.

The last key is giving. I think that I have already said a lot about the importance of giving at the beginning of this subject. When you give it's a seed that you plant! If you have planted, you shall also reap one day. Some people can never be blessed! This is because they don't like to give. God gave his only begotten son, and look how many sons and daughters he will have. By this principle of giving, he will redeem most of the human race, which had been cursed by Adam's transgression. In Exodus 25: 1 God asked Moses to ask the people for an offering. Notice that He said to Moses that He must receive the offering only from those who will give it with a good heart. You may give and never get blessed if the motives of your heart are not right. Giving is one thing, but the purpose behind your actions is what counts. You must not have any hidden motives in your head when you give! Your motive must be to be a blessing to one another. When you give, you should never expect to receive.

The Name of Jesus

The name of a person always reflects his nature, personalities and character. "I told you, and ye believed not. The works that I do in my father's name, they bear witness of me." (John 10:25).

Everything Jesus was doing when He was here on the earth, He was doing in his father's nature or name. Name in the Bible means nature. Jesus was very careful in everything he was doing, and he didn't want to do anything that would contradict the character, personality or attributes of God the father. That's why when his mind told him to turn the rock into bread he automatically condemned that desire because He knew it was not of God. There's life in the name of Jesus! There's power in the name of Jesus! If we believe in Jesus' name, we should have life and life abundantly. "But these are written, that ye might believe that Jesus is the Christ, the Son of God; and that believing ye might have life through his name" (John 20:31).

In Acts 2:38-39 Peter told the people that they had to repent of their sins, that every one of them should be baptized in the name of Jesus to receive forgiveness for their sins. Because of the supreme sacrifice that Jesus had offered to God, he had the power to clean away sins, but he cannot clean our sins if we don't come to him with repentant hearts and with regret in our hearts, knowing that we were guilty for transgressions. When we do this, his blood will clean away our sins (John 13:14). Jesus said that everything we ask in his name he would do. By that statement we know that Jesus was the true Son of God. Notice that he said "in my name." That should tell us something. That should tell us that Jesus was not a natural man whose body is governed by the law of the nature. There's no power in man, whatsoever. In the name of Jesus there is power (Prov.30:4).

There were questions asked about the Son of God. The questions were, "who ascended up into Heaven, or descended? Who gathered the wind in his fists? Who had bound the waters in a garment? Who establish all the ends of the earth? What is his name, and what is the name of his son? If thou can't tell?"

(Judges 13:18). "The angel of the Lord came to a man to give him a message from God, he asked the angel what is his name? And the angel answered who asks thus after my name; seeing it is secret." That angel of the Lord was Jesus in operation in the Old Testament! He said his name was a secret. That shows that the way of dispensation of grace was not yet opened. The secret he mentioned here, was the name Jesus. That name was not yet revealed to men. That was the reason the angel said it was a secret. It was in the name of Jesus that the way of the salvation of men had been opened. The way of man's salvation was in shadows and types, but it was opened by the crucifixion of Christ on the cross (Acts 4:12). Neither is there salvation in any other: for there is no other name under Heaven given among men whereby we must be saved. By this we know that there's a salvation in the name of Jesus. Not only by this statement but also by our own experiences. By the Holy Ghost, the name of Jesus has power (Matt. 1:21:23). Jesus had not only come to save the nation of Israel but also those in the world! The human race.

Now we have the privilege to bear the name of God by His son. We must be very careful that we do not strive in vain (Eph. 3:14-15). Paul tells us here that the name of Jesus is the family name of Heaven. We bear the name of Jesus when we receive the Holy Ghost, then we are born into the family of God. That means that we are saved only from our past sins and from the world. After we have received the baptism of the Holy Ghost, we are alive spiritually with God, but we must work for our salvation with fear and trembling. For nothing imperfect will enter in Heaven where God and Jesus are! And imperfect souls cannot go in the presence of God, in the holiest of holy! That tells us that the church must reach a point where it can produce perfection in the life of the saints. The early church was able to produce holy souls for God, but today what we see is the contrary. We hear men preaching the opposite of it. They are preaching vain salvation to people. They even preach that if someone is baptized in water, he or she is saved permanently. That there's no effort to make, and once you accept Jesus as your personal Savior, you are saved forever. That's all wrong!

Salvation has three phases. First you are saved from your past sins, from yourself and the world. This is the first phase of the salvation from yourself or the Adamic nature. Note that even though you left the world, it's still in you. You cannot go to Heaven with the world in you. So you must overcome the world within you. When you overcome the world within you, then you can say, I will be saved. This is a future term because you have still not yet entered the rest of God. When you enter the rest of God, that's when you can say, I am saved. Then your salvation is complete. Just like the children of Israel had left Egypt, but Egypt didn't leave them. Most of them perished in the desert. Then those who made it into the promised land had to fight to inherit the land. They didn't just go there and do nothing. Then their enemies would have killed them all. The name of Jesus opened the way for us. Moses was a savior for the Israelites, but he didn't tell the people that once they left Egypt they are saved forever. In fact it was much harder for them that they had to stay under the protection of God. They had to stay under the clouds, which were a symbol of the covering of God, but even under the clouds their bodies were falling and rotting in the wilderness. They had rebellious hearts.

Perfection

What is perfection? Can the church produce perfection? How will this take place? Can a human soul reach perfection or can we go to Heaven without reaching perfection? The word perfection in Greek means complete spiritual maturity (Heb. 6:1). Therefore leaving the principle of the doctrine of Christ lets us go onto perfection not laying again the foundation of repentance from the dead works and faith toward God.

First, we must know that there cannot be perfection without the judgment seat first restored in the church. The judgment seat is the power and authority of the full presence of Christ in the church, which is not a literal building, but in the group of ministers over the church. As I have said in the previous chapters, all the problems the church is facing now are because the judgment seat is not yet restored. When it is fully restored all the sinners who kept the church captive will flee away. Only the holy Christians will remain in the church. Then the church will be able to produce perfect souls for God once again.

What we see today is that sinners are leading the church, and they have no fear in their heart of God. They preach things in the morning, then commit adultery, and later on come back to preach again very hard. This is terrible. God called the leaders of the church to be examples for the saints, and the older saints in the church to be the example for the new converts in Christ. In such conditions, the church cannot produce perfect souls for God. Nothing imperfect can possibly produce perfection. This means that something must take place to change the course of the church. Restoration always begins with a group of leaders who are practicing personal holiness. When that takes place, then the Holy Spirit of God will change the course of the church, and the church will once again begin to produce perfect souls for God.

There cannot be perfection without a full doctrinal restoration. Men are preaching the word of God with their natural intellect and not by the Holy Spirit. When the Holy Ghost can finally work with men's subconscious minds, the restoration will begin. Perfection cannot begin without a personal holiness.

Without it no one can go to Heaven, because nothing impure shall enter in Heaven, where the throne of God is in the holiest of holy. God can't see anything unholy, and nothing unholy can see the face of God. Even holy angels trembled before him.

The reason why Jesus came on the earth was to sanctify a group of people by helping their souls to reach full spiritual maturity. Then he could present them as His spiritual bride to God the father. They will represent the essence of the sacrifice of Christ, the result of His supreme offering to God. They will be called the redeemers of the earth. Before this can possibly take place, there must first be a restored church with restored biblical doctrines. Only restored doctrines can produce perfection in a soul. Men's personal doctrines cannot produce spiritual souls. To have a complete victory over the flesh we need leaders according to God's plan.

We need leaders who are submitting their lives to God. Then God will restore their lives to greatness for the next great event of this age. Something great will take place, and many of us will be able to become witnesses of it.

We have seven mighty wicked spirits hidden in our souls. To get them out we need God's equipment. It's not an easy job to bring a human soul into perfection. The primitive church was able to produce perfect souls. This was because of the presence of the twelve Apostles. That's why when they all died the church had automatically fell in a profound spiritual darkness, then the postate church started.

No one can reach perfection without the knowledge and understanding of the word of God. Perfection will not come by miracle. It requires our devotion, obedience and determination to become spiritually mature in the word of God. Your pastors must not only know what he is doing, but your obedience is also required. To reach perfection our daily life with God must be controlled with circumspection. Maturity is an accumulation of facts until you gain self-control to the point where the spirit of God has total control of your whole life, body, soul and spirit (Gal. 5:16-18). No one can attain perfection without personal holiness (Eph. 5: 10-13).

No human can apprehend perfection in his or her own way. Self-righteousness cannot help us attain perfection, because it is without holiness. Our own intellectual capacities will not help us reach it. Self-denial will help us to begin our journey (Col. 3:1-10).

Setting your affection on the things from above means to focus on spiritual virtues until they become a part of your life. They will begin to develop our spiritual senses. Justice will also begin to grow in our lives, and then we can judge ourselves worthy of eternal life (Phil. 1:9-11). Fruit of spirit cannot develop without humility. When we begin to practice every little thing we learned from the word of God and don't feel proud about what we know, but use it to develop ourselves in the Lord, then we can reach perfection. To do this, a person must mentally unload his entire human desires and emotions so that he or she may become holy in their mind. He or she must become holy enough to feel God's presence every day and to receive God gifts. We don't take enough time to sanctify ourselves, lifting up our minds to God to reach a higher dimension in him, it will help us overcome sins and infirmities in our lives that keep us away from the presence of God.

No human soul can attain perfection without tribulations or fire! It was through tribulations that Paul had made it to the high calling of God. It was not only by knowledge and revelations but through tribulations (1Cor.11:23-33). We read the life of Job as a great man of God, how he had kept the faith and made it for a better resurrection (Job1:13-22). No man by any form of wisdom can attain or make it to the Bride of Christ without going first though tribulations. Fire, or tribulations, is a process of purification that God lets us go through, so we can please him. It's one thing to find the body of Christ, which is very good, but it's also good that after have we found the body of Christ to know how to grow. We can become very knowledgeable without fruit. That could cause us to perish with all the knowledge we have. That's why we must become very wise and prudent with everything we have learned and what we do with it, knowing that we are not seeking for vainglory.

There must be a spiritual growth in every Christian's life that must take place. The baptism of the Holy Ghost is not enough to make you grow (1 John 2: 12-14). Babies cannot overcome evil, even in the natural. Babies must depend on someone else for guidance, but they do not remain in the same condition forever (Isaiah 9:5).

Babies cannot bear burdens but note that Jesus did not remain a baby forever, and when he became a man, God gave him responsibilities (1 John 9: 5). When you grow, Jesus cannot be your advocate anymore. You must become sons or daughters. The sons of God are those who reach a level of perfection (Heb. 5:14).

We must reach a point where we can choose good and reject evil. This is our choice to make or not to make (Matt. 5:9). We must be a peacemaker in and out of church. We must be able to keep a good spirit in every circumstance (1 Cor. 13:1). It is the will of God that Christians must put on charity. Charity is the spirit of Christ. By the spirit of charity, Jesus was able to endure every evil test that came his way. We must be willing to suffer, and when we are suffering, it's for our own good. In every dispensation God always gives a period of time for the saints to reach perfection. The saints of the Old Testament were justified by the offering they offered to God through faith (Matt. 5:48) (Matt. 5:21-24). The saints under the dispensation of the new covenant will reach perfection through fire (1Cor. 3:12-13).

The Five Gates of the Soul

"And the Lord, God formed man of the dust of the ground and breathed into his nostrils the breath of life and man became a living soul" (Gen. 2: 7). We find out in this chapter that after God gave life into man, man then became a living soul. This means that man was created naturally, just like the beasts. The breath of life here was not a natural breath from a natural mouth, but the breath of life referred to here is the Holy Ghost. We see a beautiful picture of it after Jesus' resurrection. He blew on the twelve apostles, to receive the Holy Spirit and on the day of Pentecost, Jesus blew spiritually on the 120 that were waiting in the upper room. They received, for the first time, the power of the Holy Spirit, and all of them became living souls.

Preachers in the religious system believe that Adam was made of clay and that God blew naturally on him, and he became naturally alive. This is a big lie! God is too powerful for that! God had distinguished Adam from the other animals of the garden by giving him his Holy Spirit, which gave Adam superiority above all the beasts. That is why he was able to name single animals according to their nature.

The Holy Spirit of God gave Adam five spiritual senses. He was able to see spiritually, taste spiritually, smell spiritually, hear spiritually and touch spiritually. These five spiritual senses also represent five spiritual gates; through them you could corrupt your soul. After your spiritual birth, you become spiritually alive. You must feed your soul through these five spiritual doors. You don't have a soul; you are a soul! What you see will either give more life to your soul or kill your soul. Your ears are the mouths of your souls. What you hear will feed your soul, good or bad. If you hear trash, you are feeding your soul with trash, and that will kill your soul spiritually. If you hear spiritual things, that will give life and more strength to your soul.

Then your ears, spirituality talking, could help you taste spiritual things, but this is just a figure of your spiritual mouth. If you have a spiritual mouth, you can taste spiritual foods and if a food is good for your soul, you will know. If it's bad, you will also know because you have a spiritual mouth to taste. Your ears are to nourish your souls with either good or bad things, and a spiritual mouth is to eat spiritual foods. Your senses will communicate spiritually to tell you if a food is of God or the devil. The devil also has food for his children. Our spiritual senses help us differentiate this from preaching that comes from God. Your natural nose is a figure of your spiritual nose! You will be able to distinguish the things of the world and the things of God. You will differentiate between things that smell good and things that do not smell good. After all these comes from the sense of touch. You can touch someone's life when you become mature enough. You can touch someone with your words. Jesus told Peter that when he was converted or overcome, he would strengthen his brothers. This meant that when Peter became spiritually mature, he would be able to touch his brothers' lives. We must all develop and become full adults in the Lord. Have you ever heard a preacher who really touches your life with his words? The way they preach, the way they explain things to you in detail, really touches your life. However, we must reach a point where we can touch spiritual things ourselves.

If you read your Bible often enough: you will become skillful and sharp in the Word. Then when you open your mouth, you will be able to touch someone's life. When we begin to touch spiritual things ourselves, God will begin to trust us! A soul is a fragile substance, because after the baptism of the Holy Ghost you have a little of Jesus inside of you. You could kill your soul if you are not careful. These five gates are the only way you could corrupt your soul. These five ways are the only ways you can either strengthen or weaken your soul.

A human soul is a very complex thing. A person doesn't have a soul; he is a soul. God's plan for men is to save their souls because there is something in man that belongs to God. This is the reason why he wants to reconcile with us because man was created in his own image. Something was lost. God's plan is to restore His image again in men. This is the main reason that He sent his son among us. It was to plant the seed of everlasting life in us again. Two thousand years ago, the Son of God came down from Heaven to dwell among us, taking the shape of the human body. He had begun a work of spiritual restoration. Twelve men then became one hundred twenty and conquered the world. The primitive church had restored God's image in many men and women back there. The church of the latering saints will also restore God's image in a group of men and women but there's a great job that needs to be done. There should be a job of restoration, which must take place first. Just like the leaders of the primitive church had done. We need strong leaders, men who don't see themselves but who are willing to sacrifice for God's people. Men who are denying themselves, who are sanctifying themselves one hundred percent to God, without any compromise. Today God is seeking a group of holy men to begin this great work.

Holy men cannot be found today. It is very difficult to find a truly dedicated man of God. Money and women have blinded men's eyes. They are not seeking God with sincerity. Most of them want to get rich, living a luxurious lifestyle here on the earth. When man realizes the importance of a human soul then, God will use many of them to sanctify a people, which will judge this ungodly world.

After the baptism of the Holy Ghost, our main fight is to protect our souls in this corrupted world. If you are not watching, you could easily destroy your soul.

Preserving your soul is not an easy thing to do, especially now. The Five Gates are the only way you can pollute your soul but they are also the five ways you can spiritually feed your souls. A human soul consists of will, intellect and emotions. These three forces combine to form the human soul! A human will is the strongest one! It will not submit under the will of God. That was why Jesus said, not my will but "thy will be done." It is not easy to humble your will in anything. The human will can either block its way to God, or open the way for you. Your intellect helps you accumulate knowledge of the word of God. You could become strong in the lord. The emotions and motivations are the spiritual part of the soul. Your emotions help you connect with the Holy Spirit. Your emotions help motivate you and transport you to a higher spiritual level, where you can have spiritual contact with God through the Holy Ghost.

A human being is formed in three parts: body, soul and spirit. The body part is where all the instincts and natural appetites and desires come from. The soul is the real you, and the spirit is the mysterious part of a human. Your spirit is inside your soul. Your spirit is not your soul! Your soul influences your spirit; it controls your spirit. It is under the command of the soul. Your emotions and motivations are part of your spirit.

When you receive the Holy Ghost, it renews your soul and your spirit in God, but it is only a seed. A seed must have very good care in order to grow. After receiving the baptism of the Holy Ghost, you receive the seed of everlasting life and under intensive care it can grow in God's image. Just like a natural seed, when you plant it, you must water it regularly, until a little tree springs up. After the little tree comes up from the ground, you must take good care of it until it becomes a giant tree, it's roots growing deep down in the ground, gaining strength from the energy of the sun and all the minerals from the ground. It is the same for a human soul. If you don't take care of it, it will never grow and develop.

Seven Angels

In our time, God has a ministry that is operating in a very high spiritual dimension. The word *angel* in Greek simply means messenger. God has human messengers in our time. Some of them are also rebellious messengers. In the Old Testament, God used to send angels on missions to earth to warn or to give messages to different people in Israel. Then he used many prophets, but in our days God is using human messengers to give His word to His people. It's the responsibility of the seventh angel, not by its own might but by the power of the word of God. They will destroy their wicked works with the sound of the spiritual trumpet. The ministry of the seven thousand years will destroy the rest of their works by plagues.

It will be the heavenly Jerusalem that will rule with Christ for a thousand years. God had a secret for the natural Jewish people that had divided into three different parts: first, a priesthood kingdom; second, a holy nation; and third, a kingly, sacerdotal, elected nation (Exodus 19:5-6). However, notice that God said only if they obeyed his divine law. This was a high calling for the nation of Israel (1 Peter 2:9-10) (Rev 1: 4). One of the principal desires that the Lord had was to have a people on the earth to bear his divine nature (Rev20: 6).

Our greatest fight today is to keep our names in the book of life. Your sins can separate you from God's favor, just like the nation of Israel. In general terms, a minister produces an overcome people. The seven churches, in general terms, represent the spiritual condition of the latering (Rev 1:19-21) (Rev 2:1). Those who are overcome must also overcome false religions, the spirit of iniquity, and all the works of the flesh (Rev. 2:12).

Notice that in each letter written to the churches Jesus has a different aspect and each aspect symbolizes something different (Rev. 3:1) (Rev. 3:21) (Psalms 5:3).

The prayers of the saints of the early church represented the sacrifice of the morning (Ex. 29:28-39). This represents the sacrifice of the night because we know that there must be two sacrifices that must take place for the Bride of Christ to be completed (Psalms 141:2-3) (Rev. 6:9-11) (Rev. 4:1).

The door must be opened first in order for the blood of the saints to be avenged. This door is open in our time (Rev. 6:11) (Rev. 3:21) (Rev. 8:1). The accomplishment of Revelations 4, chronologically speaking, is when something is closed, and when it is fulfilled, God will collect the last member of the Bride and there will be a silence on the earth.

The twenty-four elders are a symbol of the Bride of Christ. The four beasts are also a symbol of the Bride. This is a symbolic number that explains the Bride of Christ (Rev. 8:1). One half-hour equals seven and one half years. The seven angels are a symbol of the Bride of Christ. The seven trumpets are a symbol of the messages that will be preached (Heb. 9:11).

All of the spiritual virtues that were in Jesus show that he was a spiritual tabernacle. In the natural tabernacle the priests used to sprinkle upon the utensils, but on the day of Pentecost Jesus did a perfect sprinkling upon the 120 in the upper room with the Holy Ghost.

The perfumes represent our attitudes, our good comportment, including our divine love (1 John 3:1-2) (1John 3:15-16) (Luke 14:25). Jesus means those who don't want you serve God must be hated. It means to stay away from them (John 3:16 the supreme love) (Gal. 5:22 the result of true love) (1 Cor. 13:1-2 nature of Christ) (Rev. 5:8).

In every dispensation, a seal was opened before. In the Old Testament, everything used to be in types and shadows. Jesus was the only one who had the qualities to open the seals. The revelation of the word of God begins to reveal the glory of God manifested.

It shows a righteous judgment that will take place (Rev. 8:6) (Rev. 15).

The seven plagues describe that the Bride of Christ is not on the earth (Rev. 3:21). God will begin to judge the earth after the last member of the bride is in, when the Bride is completed. (Rev. 6:11).

Those who are standing upon the transparent sea are those of the Bride of the Lord Jesus Christ. The sea is a symbol of the people left upon the earth after the battle of Armageddon. Their conditions will be transparent. They will be pure. Only those who are not taking the mark of the beast will remain (Rev. 4:4).

The fact that there are 24 elders is another symbolic number that describes the Bride of Christ. Eyes before and behind mean that there were prophets who had the understanding of the Old and the New Testaments. The Bride will have eyes on the present, the past and the future (Rev. 7:9) (Rev. 15:3-4).

The song of the lamb and Moses is the harmony of the Old and New Testaments manifested (Rev. 5:9). This chapter proves that everybody is called to be part of the Bride but only a few will be elected (2 Cor. 15:2) (Rev. 21:22) (Rev. 15:5) (Rev. 21:16). That they are equal means that every member of the Bride will be equal in authority and power; they will have the same angelic bodies (Acts 15:13-16).

The name of God is a mystery. This mystery was first revealed to Corneil the pagan when Peter laid hands upon him and his family. It was a mystery for the Jews. There are also many kinds of angels in the third heaven where God and Jesus are. They are created with a spiritual substance that allows them to travel everywhere, through the air. They could resist any temperature. They could walk through fire. They have full power and authority over nature. There are also human angels in the second heavenly condition.

The restoration of the latering church will be paradise restored on earth. The ministers operating in the church will be like angels in the second heavenly condition. However, the seven angels are a symbol of the Bride of Christ. The number of overcomers is 14,000 in general. The seven plagues will fall upon the earth in the millennial reign of Christ (Rev. 8:8).

These verses deal with the Armageddon. People who will face these catastrophic events will curse God with their mouths. This is the great tribulation period. (Rev. 9:1) Having fallen from Heaven here is not referring to where God and Jesus are, but to a spiritual condition. They had fallen from their spiritual condition (Rev. 9:13) (Rev. 11:15). This is end of all kingdoms of the earth (Rev. 10:7).

Shepherd

What is a shepherd? What are the characteristics of a true shepherd? How do we recognize a true shepherd? In John 10:11, Jesus said, "I am a good shepherd: a good shepherd giveth his life for the sheep." This is the key factor here! Many preachers may claim to be pastors, or shepherd but if they are not willing to even give their lives for you, then you know that they are not good shepherds. If a pastor only sees your money and what you can do for only him, then you know he is not a good pastor.

A good shepherd must have certain qualities in himself before taking the office or the responsibility of a pastor. Paul says, in 1 Tim. 3:2, that a bishop then must be blameless, the husband of one wife, vigilant, sober, have good behavior, be given to hospitality, apt to teach, not given to wine, not greedy of filthy lucre, patient, not a brawler, not covetous, and one that ruleth well his own house, having his children in subjection with all gravity. These are the qualities that you must find in a shepherd. If not, he is not a true shepherd! In John 10:1-2, Jesus says, "verily, verily I say unto you he that entered not by the door into the sheepfold, but climbeth up some other way, the same is a thief and a robber. But he that entereth in by the door is the shepherd of the sheep." Many so-called pastors are thieves because they have not entered by the door but they entered by a religious headquarter. A good shepherd should not see his own personal interests. He should see the interests of the people.

First, a shepherd is a watchman, a protector and a provider. A shepherd will not have a five-bedroom house with three baths when his people are renting. A shepherd sees the interest of his sheep first and then himself. A shepherd is the steward of God. He must not be someone who lives a full and luxurious lifestyle.

A true shepherd owns nothing on the earth because he knows that everything on the earth will someday fade away. When you are a true shepherd, your sheep should not be in desperate need while you are living in abundance. That is why David said, in Psalms 23:1, "the Lord is my shepherd. I shall not want." because he knew that God would always take care of his needs.

A shepherd should take care of God's people. He is the guardian of God's people. A shepherd must feed the sheep (John 21:16). Jesus told Peter that if he loved him then he must feed his sheep.

We are not speaking of natural food or natural sheep. A pastor should be like a shepherd and the saints he is leading represent his sheep. He must feed them with the word of God. He must take care of the saints better than he takes care of himself. He should not let other false preachers influence his people. He should not let false doctrines get into their souls, because God will severely punish him for that.

False preachers represent wolves who will destroy the sheep. A true shepherd should have the eyes to identify wolves when they get into the pasture. A good shepherd always wants to keep the sheep together. He will not divide them. If a preacher is preaching division then you know he is not of God.

God is a God of unity, a God of love. He loves those who are working in love and peace with each other. Many preachers know how to upset people more than they know how to comfort them. They know how to use the word of God to make people miserable. When someone is out there working very hard, his or her spirit is already beat up with the stress of the day. When they come to church later, they must leave with hope and with their faith strengthened, not weakened.

We must be able to make people crave to hear the word of God. When Jesus was here on earth, his words brought forth hope and happiness in the people's hearts.

\When they didn't see him, they looked for him everywhere. This was because of the joy he brought to their hearts and the hope he gave them. They had to respect Him and honor him. The job of a true shepherd, is to make people feel secure and safe under their leadership. A true shepherd's main vision is to see God's people saved. He should not use the word of God to beat them or wound their hearts. If a shepherd does, that he will face God's terrible judgment one day.

David said, in Psalms 23:4, "thy rod and thy staff, they comfort me." We know the rod he was speaking about here is not a natural rod but a picture of the word of God. Building people's faith in Christ is not a simple job! It requires wisdom and the spirit of support to do it. That is why a true shepherd must have all of his five spiritual senses fully developed. Men who can present themselves as models for the people. Building people's faith in Christ is one of the most difficult jobs in the world. That is why a weak person cannot be a shepherd. It must be someone who genuinely loves God and is willing to give up his life for God's people. A shepherd must know that he is nothing and that he can't do anything without God. He is just a vessel in the hand of God.

To build people spiritually, you need to be spiritually higher than the people. You cannot be on the same spiritual level with them and expect to change their lives. It is impossible. That is why a true shepherd is constantly seeking God's guidance, in order to lead the people with integrity and wisdom.

A shepherd must meditate and fast constantly. They must have a plan to help the people reach spiritual maturity. When you have a plan, you communicate the plan. It's a question of controlling the people in all situations. A leader can limit his authority by the way he uses it. After you establish the controlling principles, then you must enforce the control (Deut. 34:9 the sanctification of Joshua to succeed Moses). In 1 Tim 4:4 it says not to neglect the gift, which is in you. Wisdom and strength produce stability (Joshua 1:6-9). You must know that wisdom is not salvation if it is not properly applied. Earthly wisdom can become a destructive force. After you tell the people what to do, you must go back and reinvestigate to be sure that everything is in order. A true leader must also meditate on the people he is leading. Keeping every individual in mind, he must consider and calculate the needs of the people. He must make a list of everything, all the problems the people have with one another, but he must not concentrate on the problems. He should think of solutions to help the people. He must consider all the things that God wants him to accomplish. He must know the needs of the people. The people need a spiritual covering that will determine their spiritual destiny. Our whole lives depend on that. A shepherd must teach the people how to cooperate and have the fear of God in everything they are doing. It must be done for the edification of the church in general.

A pastor or shepherd is a spiritual covering for the people or the saints, under his ministry. Therefore he must himself have Christ as his spiritual covering, and we know that God the father is the spiritual covering for Christ (1 Cor. 11:3). This divine order will shape the people's progress and destiny. Their whole lives depend on the spiritual covering they have (Num. 19:15). There are two different vessels in the kingdom of God! In a common sense, some vessels refer to humans. A human life without the covering of God is unclean unto God. On the other hand, a covered vessel is a clean vessel in God's eyes: honored vessels and dishonored vessels. Any uncovered pit will always pick up impurities (Isa. 28:20) (Psalms 32:1). A pastor should have his sins well covered by the blood of Jesus and should be able to keep himself clean in order to maintain an effective ministry approved by God. If not, he will be a worthless vessel in the kingdom of God.

Faith

There are three kinds of faith. The first is the kind of faith that people have in their regular life, like the faith to have a job, or the faith to do something or accomplish something in life. This is natural faith. Most people in the world do have natural faith. They operate on an earthly level, doing things and accomplishing things that have nothing to do with God. The second kind of faith is reasonable faith. This is the faith that people have to have the things that they can see and can find justification for it to be done. When someone sees that something can be done, they will believe they can do it, and they will do it. This is what we call reasonable faith.

The third kind of faith is supernatural faith. This is the faith to accomplish impossible things. (Heb. 11:1) The Greek word for this faith is *pistis*. It means belief, faith, trust and confidence. Whatever people believe is what their hopes will be. Supernatural faith is an absolute substance that cannot be explained with anything else. It is the highest level of faith. It is not only the faith to find the things you need, but it's the faith to save your souls. This faith is a vehicle to carry you into your destination. The standards of the world offer a measure of comfort and prosperity, but the divine standard of God sometimes offers suffering, unpopularity, discomfort, humility and even death. Our faith is against the worldly system. Our faith gives certain steps to follow (Heb, 11:26-28) (Dan. 3:30-31). Men, referred to in these passages disobeyed a powerful king with his powerful army, a king who was vigilant and very wicked, just to obey an invisible God they didn't see with their eyes. We as Christians today, are lacking faith, and we are like a prisoner who has the key of a prison, yet remains imprisoned by his doubts.

Faith defies pleasures of the world. In everything man does, he wants a reward for it. He always expects that after, there will be pleasure without end. There are two kinds of pleasure. The first kind refers to the temporary pleasures of the world, at the end of which is always death and deception.

The second is the everlasting pleasure of God, which had no end. Faith makes the present substance become future substance. The word *hupostasis* in Greek translates to the word substance, just as Christ was a substance of God the Father (Heb. 3:14). Faith gave us a foundation that is very sure, that we can stand up on (Rom. 8:24-25) (Heb. 11:13-17) (Eph. 2:8). The word evidence is, in Greek, *elenches* and means conviction. We invest our lives in a substance that we do not see with our natural eyes. Our faith goes on, even to the impossible. It's the conviction of things that we do not see but that do exist (John 20:29) (Rom. 10:17-20) (1 Cor. 1:21).

There is a degree of faith we call faith of reason. It's the reason behind your belief. What pushes someone to believe something? Is the reason righteous or unrighteous? "Therefore being justified by faith, we have peace with God, through our Lord Jesus Christ: by whom also we have access by faith into his grace, wherein we stand and rejoice in hope of the glory of God." (Rom. 5:1). Verse 3 says, "and not only so but we glory in tribulations also: knowing that tribulations worketh patience. And patience hope: and hope maketh not ashamed because the love of God is shed abroad in our hearts by the Holy Ghost, which giveth unto us." Faith is not only used to get what you want, but it is the substance that causes us to believe, even though we don't see it with our natural eyes. We have tasted the glory of the life to come. We have experienced it and we feel it in our souls.

What we are preparing for is the day of the great tribulation period. God will test our faith, just like He did for the early church. "Women received their dead raised to life again: And others were tortured, not accepting deliverance, that they might obtain a better resurrection: And others had trials of cruel mockings and scourgings, yea moreover of bonds and imprisonment. They were stoned, they were sown asunder, were tempted, and were slain with the sword: they wandered about in sheepskins and goatskins; being destitute, affected, tormented; of whom the world was not worthy: they wandered in desserts, and in mountains, and in dens and caves of the earth." (Heb. 11:35-36). Verses 39 says, "these all, having obtained a good report through faith, received not the promise." What we ask ourselves today is can we pass all of the tests to come? Because many getting in the way don't really understand what they are getting into when we talk of getting into the narrow way of God. It is true that the end of it is life everlasting, but how many of us will make it to the end? Will we still be standing when the final test comes? These people in Heb. 11:35, had gone through all of these terrible things and never attained the promise.

Those of us who live in this present time are very fortunate. We had the promise because the promise was the Holy Ghost! However, we are not going to get there without going through the fire of God, which will qualify our souls to enter the presence of God. Flesh and blood cannot enter the presence of God. This means that our natural, physical bodies cannot see God. That is why our souls need to be perfected and purified. Then God will give us a new body that our souls can dwell in. That angelic body will be the rest of God. When we have the body, then Jesus will present us before God as his Bride.

The word faith, in its real sense, means to be rooted in the knowledge of the word of God because it takes knowledge to be rooted. Faith is not only believing in God for our natural needs; it's more likely for our spiritual needs. Faith is the foundation of every follower of Christ, who has the desire to be in the Bride of Christ. Faith is not only believing. We should also have enough faith to save our souls. Faith is our tool to overcome temptation. It is a virtue needed to operate in the kingdom of God and to heal the sick, both naturally and spiritually. It is by faith that we can destroy the work of the devil and the flaming desires that sometimes come to destroy our souls.

There is a big difference between faith and the power of the human will. We must be able to distinguish between faith and the power of the will. The power of the will has its limit because it works for the flesh (Heb. 11:8). Abraham had nothing visible on which he could put his faith. He held his faith even though it took a long time for God to fulfill the promise, he gave him a son and the secret of it was that Abraham had kept the faith.

The Effect of Traditions on the Church

Jesus had warned his Disciples about the false doctrines of the Pharisees and the Sadducees (Matt. 16:6-12). They had a form of righteousness when they abandoned the written law to practice the oral law. They had created these laws for their own self-righteousness. After a certain time, they became so corrupt and spiritually blind that God himself decided to put an end to that system. So in 70 A.D. they all perished from the siege on Jerusalem by the Roman Empire.

Nimrod had originated the root of many false doctrines after the great flood. He was able to provide safety for the people from being victimized by wild beasts. He used many traps and tricks to kill the violent wild beasts because of his skills and talents, the people believed in him. After awhile, he asked to be worshipped as a god (Gen. 11:1-9). God came down and confused them, so the people would not be able to accomplish their goals. That is exactly what is going on in the religious world today. The people wanted to build Nimrod a spiritual time worshipping center to unite in the flesh, and God came down and confused their language so that they would not be able to accomplish their evil goals. What they really wanted to do was to produce the image of the first beast. They were not able to reproduce God's image because they did not have the spirit of God in them in order to do so.

The church of the body of Christ had fallen into a profound spiritual darkness from 311 A.D. to 538 A.D., which was the period of the Black Horse. In the period of time starting from 70 A.D. to 311 A.D., they destroyed the church's spiritual fruit. Man's religions and traditions changed the course of the church of the Body of Christ. Man's ambitions of power brought division. The people established a system where they could create more false doctrines (Rev. 6:5). Wicked emperors ruled during the period of 311 A.D. to 538 A.D. There were no interpretations of the word of God. There were no spiritual activities at all. The balance was a picture of the political power mixed with religious power. The result of this was very catastrophic. Many saints lost heir lives.

In this present time, there are more traditions and confusions in the church than ever before! There are so many personal interpretations of the Bible, which bring us to a place where we can easily get more confused. Where did all these things come from? Some may ask why did God let all these things happen?

There are two great mysteries in the Bible: the mystery of iniquity and the mystery of godliness, or the secret church of Jesus Christ. In the Old Testament the priests used to teach the kingdom of God and predicted the coming of the messiah, but they did not preach about the kingdom of God under the name of the church. That is why Paul had called it a mystery. After the fall Adam and Eve, they were taken out of the Garden of Eden. After Eve gave birth to Cain and Abel, two lines had begun, the righteous line and the unrighteous line (Gen. 11:4).

After the great flood, Nimrod built his name as a mighty hunter, so the people would worship him as a god. They rejected the true invisible and eternal God, the creator of mankind. Nimrod built a strong civil and religious power mixed together to create the greatest confusion on the earth up to this time. He was the author of the trinity doctrine. Later on he became the sun god, and his wife Semuramus became the Queen of Heaven (Ezek. 8:13:18). When Nimrod died his wife Semuramus gave birth to a son. She said that it was Nimrod reincarnated through her. So the people also worshipped the son. This gives us the triangle that formed the trinity doctrine. In all these things that had taken place, God had preserved a righteous line until Abraham (Heb. 11:8-10). From then there has always been two lines, the righteous line and the unrighteous line.

The same way that God put an end to the corrupt activities of men in the past, is the way he will put an end to the perverted activities and corruption of the men in our time. God is separating his people today by the church of the Body of Christ. When that work is completely fulfilled, there will be the judgment of God on this earth. All the ungodly shall perish without mercy. The Roman Catholic Church is the source of all the false traditions we have from the fallen of the primitive church up to now. That is why it is pictured as the woman sitting on the seven-headed beast with a golden cup, filled with abominations in her hand (Rev. 17:3-4). We naturally know that there has never been an actual beast with seven natural heads, but the beast refers to the seven old empires, which became the foundation of the Roman Catholic Church. Of course, the woman symbolized the Roman Catholic Church! And of course, the golden cup in her hand is the Bible. The abominations are the false doctrines and the traditions they had added to the church. They created damage that it took God about two thousand years to repair. They destroyed more saints than any other opposing institution that ever existed. They added many false doctrines that were very difficult to remove, because they also became a force that kept the whole church captive for more than 1,260 years. These years were the period of the deepest spiritual darkness that ever existed in the history of the church.

Now great light begins to shine again. The sun of righteousness is rising again. The lattering church is getting ready to once again to give its fruit. God will judge this world and like Babylon the great mother of all the harlots. Something great is about to take place in our time and most of us, in this present age, will have a chance to see the manifestation of the Son of God. Healing and restoration will come again! The church of the Body of Christ will be glorious once again!

Humility

In Matt. 18:1-4 the Disciples of Christ came to join him and asked him" who is the greatest in the kingdom of God?" In verse 2 Jesus answered them by calling a little child and placing him in the midst of them saying, "verily I say unto you, if someone is not converted and become like little children, he cannot enter the Kingdom of God." I verse 4 Jesus says "whosoever therefore shall humble himself as the little child, the same is greatest in the Kingdom of Heaven."

Why do you think Jesus made that illustration for the Disciples? It is because at that time none of the Disciples were humble. Jesus wanted to show them that without humility, no one would make it. The Jewish people were naturally proud, and it was because of the proud spirit that most of them missed such great opportunity under the dispensation of grace.

The next great lesson that Jesus gave the Disciples was when he took water and a towel and began to wash the Disciples' feet. (John 13:5). However, the key verse is in verses 13-15, "ye call me master and Lord: And ye say well; for so I am. If I then your Lord and Master, have washed your feet; ye also ought to wash one another's feet." This was an allegory and a lesson. It doesn't mean that Jesus wanted the Disciples to literally wash each other's feet. It means to put on charity for one another, to manifest the spirit of support for each other.

Another great lesson we have is in Matt. 15:24-28: " I am not sent but unto the lost sheep of the house of Israel." In verse 25 the woman then fell to Jesus' feet and begins to worship him. Jesus told the woman in verse 26 that it was not good to take the children's bread and to cast it to the dogs. In verse 27 the woman's response touched Jesus' heart. She says truthfully, "Lord, let the dogs eat the pieces, which fall from their masters' table." Then Jesus said, "O woman, great is thy faith: be it unto thee even as thou wilt." This is a great lesson of humility. Even though Jesus had called her dog, she still persisted. She knew that Jesus was able to help her. It takes a great deal of humility and courage to remain positive after being insulted. Not too many people have enough courage and faith to do that. Jesus never realized that he could find such humility and faith in the ungodly world. That woman caused Jesus and even God to change their minds about those in the world. Jesus realized that there are lamb-like people in the world. He realized there are sheep lost in the world that he must redeem out of the world. Even among the religious Jews, Jesus could not find such tremendous humility. It is not something you can find even in the church.

These so-called Christians today are arrogant and proud; I don't see how they can possibly go to Heaven. Jesus is our real example of humility. "Let the mind be in you, which was also in Christ Jesus, who, being in the form of God, thought it robbery to be equal with God: But made himself of no reputation, and took upon him the form of a servant, and was made in the likeness of men: And being found in fashion as a man, he humble himself, and became obedient unto death, even the death of the cross" (Phil 2:5). Jesus' humility had caused God to give him a name above all names, and became our perfect example. That's why he is the head of the church because he had set the example for us to follow. The Bible says that God had highly exalted him above all (Phil 2:9). "Humble yourselves under the hands of God, and he shall lift you up" (James 4:10).

The main reason people don't want to humble themselves is because they don't want to suffer humiliation in the flesh. If we don't want to suffer in the flesh, then we will never finish with sin in our lives. "The fear of the Lord is the instruction of wisdom; and before honor is humility"(Prov. 15: 33). Everyone wants to great in the Kingdom of God, but no one wants to suffer. The Bible says that Jesus suffered and was humiliated by his own people. If Jesus is our example, then we must follow his ways. People think that going to church and learning how to become religious will same them, but there's a pattern to reach perfection. There is no perfection without tribulations, which is a symbol of fire, spiritually speaking. How will God truly know that we are Gold, if he doesn't test us? Fire will always come to purify us, and if we are gold, we will become pure. If we are not, we will be burned. Humility proceeds glory No one wants to be humiliated. No one wants to be humbled. Without it, we know for sure that is impossible to make it. Jesus had humiliated himself to obey the will of God. That's why God exalted him. It's because he had a goal, and a vision. He wanted to create the way for us to follow. The way is now open for us, but it is up to us if we are willing to follow his footsteps. In our time, many are pretending that they want to pay the price, but no one wants to die. When I say die, I mean death of the flesh. In Col. 3:5 Paul says, "mortify therefore your members, which are upon the earth," and he gave a entire list of things Christians should not do. He says that we must give up these things in order for us to become alive with Christ. In Matt. 5:3 Jesus said, "blessed are the poor in spirit for the Kingdom of Heaven is for them." What we see today is that people who call themselves Christians are very rich in their own spirit, characters and personalities. We ask ourselves how these people will inherit the Kingdom of Heaven. "Whosoever exalteth himself shall be abased and he who humbleth himself shall be exalted" (Luke 14:11). That is the reason Jesus had been exalted because he had humbled himself under god's authority. "Being found in fashion as a man, he humbled himself and became obedient unto death even the death of the cross. "Therefore, God also hath highly exalted him and gave him a name which is above every name" (Phi. 2:8). "god resists to proud but giveth grace unto the humble" (James 4:6). Prov. 6:16 says that the six things that God hates includes a proud look and a lying tongue. "Humble yourself under the mighty hand of God that he may exalt you in due time" (1 Peter 5:6).

When God wants you to be humbled he will expose you to all kinds of humiliations until he gets you where he wants you toe. Some people are predestined to fulfill God's purpose. The only thing that holds them up is pride. God will use all his power to bring you into humility and obedience.

The greatest danger is to become a preacher with pride in your life. You will create problems and defeat the church because words have the power to create or destroy. Your pride will reflect in your preaching, and you will pass your prideful spirit to people. That is why when God truly calls someone to be a vessel of the righteousness for him he will purge these things out of your life. Imagine how many proud preachers are out there preaching, and they are creating the beast image in the people's lives.

It is hard and very painful to deny ourselves. If we don't deny ourselves, however we cannot please God. To please god we must be willing to undergo his fire, which will purify us. The fire of God is the trial and tribulations that will come our way to purify our live.

The Mystery of Death

Is man created to die? The questions we can ask ourselves today is why do man die, and what really causes man to die? "And the Lord command the man, saying of every tree and the garden they could freely eat, but of the tree of the knowledge of good and evil thou shalt not eat of it: for in the day they did, they shall surely die" Gen.2:16-17).

The word *surely* means completely, both spiritually and physically. Now the question we should ask is what kind of tree was the tree of knowledge, good or evil? Was it a natural tree or a symbolic tree? The answer is that all of the other trees in the garden were indeed natural trees. However, two trees were symbolic trees. They were the tree of life and the tree of knowledge of good and evil. According to the law of procreation, every tree shall reproduce according to its own kind. We see this taking place before our eyes literally every day. The reason that the two trees were not literal trees is because we do not know of a tree called the tree of life or the tree of knowledge good and evil today. If such trees really existed, then we would also see their literal fruits of reproduction. We know for a fact that these two trees were symbolic If they were not literal, then what are they? The tree of knowledge good and evil was Adam, and the tree of life was Jesus. In other words, God told Adam not to be self-dependent. You don't depend on God for guidance when you are eating from the tree of knowledge of good and evil. That's exactly what Adam and Eve did. They agreed together not to rely on God for guidance. They wanted to build a kingdom with their own image reflected in it. They saw what the animals of the garden did to reproduce according to their own kind, so they did it too. "We know that we have passed from death unto life because we love brethen. He that loveth not his brother abidetth in death" (1 John 3:14). In 1 John 5:24-25 Jesus said, "verily, verily, I say unto you he that hear my word and believe on him that sent me hath everlasting life and shall not come to into death but passed from the death unto life. Verily, verily, I say unto you, the hour is coming and now is when the dead shall heat the voice of the Son of God and they shall live." All these verses show us the evidence of spiritual death.

The baptism of the Holy Spirit gives us life into our souls. That's why it's very important to receive the baptism of the Holy Spirit after our conversion. In Rom. 5:12 Paul says, "wherefor, as by one man sin entered into the world, and death by sin and so death passed upon all men, for all that have sinned." Death here is both physical and spiritual. When our subconscious mind is in complete ignorance of the word and the spirit of God, we are dwelling in spiritual death. The danger of the spiritual death is that any time physical death occurs, you are completely perished forever, with no hope of a resurrection.

When you examine death, you will see that God did not create man to die. Note that there was a warning given to the first man. Adam was not to eat from the tree of knowledge good and evil. So what really brought death upon mankind was first, disobedience and the evil knowledge they had from the beginning. Everything evil had its fruits, and the fruit produced death. That's why God did not want man to go that way. So he advised man not to do so, for if he did he would surely die.

Some leaders preach that human souls are immortal. The word proves that they are all liars because God cannot lie. He said if he ate from the tree he shall truly die, and he did. The word of God is absolute and powerful. That's why God had warned Adam about not being self-dependent, in everything that he was going to do, he must use God spiritual laws.

Man cannot be self-dependent because there's nothing in him that would help him to live forever. The re's no spiritual substance whatsoever in man that would allow him to be. So when man withdraws himself from God's spiritual laws he dies. Adam was created in God's image, which means he was created with the spiritual virtues and the attributes of God. When he sins against the law of God, he dies. Anytime spiritual death occurs natural death will follow, so the only way that Adam could live forever was to continue to live on earth is to eat from the tree of life. This means to live by the law of the spirit of life, which is in Christ Jesus, the tree of life. The law of spirit of life was always in one place and that was in Jesus, even from the beginning.

After Adam fell, he created that law of sin and death. "Therefore as by the offense of one, judgment came upon all men to condemnation, even so by the righteousness of one the free gifts came upon all men unto justification of life" (Rom. 5:18). " For the law of the spirit of life in Christ Jesus hath made me free from the law of sin and death" (Rom. 8:2). "For the wages of sin is death but the gift of God is eternal life through Jesus Christ our Lord" (Rom. 6:23).

Death is two-dimensional. The most apparent form of death is very common to the human race. The word for it is *Viz,* which translates as physical death, but there is another form of death. That is the spiritual death. It is much more terrible than physical death. When someone gets cut off, they are dead even though they may be physically alive. The Greek word *tartaroo* also translates hell, which describes a spiritual condition. "When Lust hath conceived it bringeth sin, and when sin when it is finished bring forth death" (James 1:15). This kind of death is spiritual death. He cannot lie. Men are proven to be liars from the beginning. When God says something, it will be fulfilled.

Death is not a pleasant thing. In fact, death is the ugliest thing to ever exist. The most humiliating thing that men are experiencing is the fruit of disobedience and the reward of sin. The secret of everlasting life had been revealed in Jesus Christ the Son of God. The sacrifice of Jesus Christ had reopened the way to everlasting life. Only those who come to him can receive the gift of everlasting life in their souls. God made no provision for human physical bodies. That's why he had promised other bodies to those who overcame sin their lives. The human body was condemned to die, since sin was condemned in the body. So it dies along with all of the evil desires, natural appetites and evil instincts that dwell in the body. That's why it's Impossible for the human body to live forever. Now if Adam had never sinned, God would never condemn sin the body. Therefore, the body would live forever, as long as man stayed in harmony with the law of life.

Adam was supposed to be a shadow of rest for the entire human race, but by his own offense he produced a shadow of death instead.

God created Adam first, and through him, there was supposed to be a holy race. Since man cannot destroy God's eternal plan, he sent his own son, in the likeness of man, to restore the plan of salvation (Eph. 2:1-10). "Every sin that dwells in us is a shadow of death" (James 1:13-15) (Gen. 3:6). It was eve's imagination that has caused her to sin against God's Law.

There were three kinds of shadows. First there is a shadow that produces rest, justice and everlasting life (Jesus). Second, there is a shadow that produces death and third, false religious cults, and their leaders also represent the shadow of death. Their doctrines produce death. They cannot produce life, for they dwell under the shadow of death because of ignorance. They are slaves of sin and corruption (Rom. 1:18).

Resistance Against Sins

"Submit yourselves therefore to God, resist the devil, and he will flee from you" (James 4:7). No one can resist the corruption and the pleasures of this world if he or she doesn't receive the baptism of the Holy Ghost. The Holy Ghost's baptism is the power that can help us live above sin. No human, by any form of philosophy or any personal effort, can live above sin without the power of the Holy Ghost in his life. "We are not wrestled against flesh and blood but against the principalities, against powers and rulers of the world of darkness" ((Eph. 6:12).

We cannot resist against these powerful forces that rule the human race without a higher supernatural force, because these are the powerful spirits that governs the entire human race. When we receive the power of the Holy Ghost, we have what it takes to resist these forces. "As many as received him to them he gave power to become the Son of God" (John 1:12). The power referred to here is the Holy Spirit. Then he says in verse 13, "which were born not blood nor of the will of the flesh nor of the will of man but of God." Resistance means not only resisting sin but also more likely resisting personal infirmities in our lives. The bloodiest fight we have to face is the fight to overcome temptation in our lives. The only way we can possibly do that is to have proper biblical knowledge. "Let no man say when he is tempted, I am tempted of God, for God cannot tempteth with evil, neither tempeth he any man, but every man is tempted when he is drawn away of his own lust and enticed" (James 1:13-14).

Our temptations come from the Adamic nature we inherited from Adam and Eve. Adam and his wife Eve were in the Garden of Eden in a perfect spiritual condition. Then temptation came, and both of them had failed to overcome it.

After the fall of Adam, Job was the first human being who had to go through fire and was able to come out pure as gold. That's why God redeemed him from his sins and gave a chance of a better resurrection. He was the first among men who genuinely had such faith and trust of God (Job1:14-22).

The Apostle Paul was one of the most wonderful and powerful Apostles. He had to go through many trials that helped him overcome many sins and personal infirmities in his life.

Jesus had to constantly cast out evil imaginations that came in his mind by the hundreds. He was able to overcome every single one of them without compromising with any of them. He had to keep his faith of his father to overcome temptations in his life. He partially inherited the Adamic nature from Mary. He had to overcome that part in his life. He was tempted in everything, yet without sin.

To become holy, a person must unload his human desires and emotions, so that he or she may become holy in his or her mind and can think positively. We must become holy enough to feel the mighty presence of God in a higher dimension and in a higher experience.

We have often enough or long enough not lifted our minds, which constantly dwell in the secret place of the most high, to overcome sin infirmities that keep us from entering in the presence of God. Human carnal minds are compared to a snake. Because of the variation of its subtleties, God calls us out of the world, baptizing us with his Holy Spirit, which give us power to live above sin. We must train our minds to think right. It's only by training our minds to obey the law of God that we can succeed in this battle.

We may receive the power of the Holy Ghost, but if we don't take even extra steps to control the Adamic nature, we can find ourselves doing things that even worse than before conversion. That's why the Adamic nature is deceiving even great leaders of the church. It's not like they want to fall, but because they take the Adamic nature lightly It deceives them. Some of them think they are very strong in the Lord and that nothing can shake them up. Next thing they know, they are on their knees, falling before the great giant, the Adamic nature. This is because they do not put a limit in certain things. A true man of God must limit himself from certain things. If not, he can easily fall into the devil's traps. It's like playing with gasoline and matches. Next, a great flame of fire consumes their souls. A man of God, or a dedicated church member, must be very wise and prudent with the Adamic nature. Not only in one aspect but also in every aspect. You must keep that nature under constant surveillance. That's why Jesus said to pray and watch the adversary. He meant the Adamic nature.

As I have said in the previous chapters, if you have an adversary, the only way you can destroy him is to first locate where he hides. If you don't know where he's hiding, then you are subject to be invaded at any time or at any moment. We need to know the Adamic nature, how it functions and how it attacks most of the time. The area where you may think you are strong is where it could destroy you easily. No one should trust the Adamic nature. Never expose yourself to the Adamic nature. If you lean how to control the flow of your thoughts, you will get control of the Adamic nature. It operates through your mind, your natural appetites, and your instincts. It could trick you only in those areas.

The True Characteristic of Goats and Lambs

Sheep are lambs. Therefore they have several characteristics and qualities that reveal a divine nature. That is why God loves lambs and hates goats. A lamb has an obedient nature. It never rebels under any circumstances. They are meek in spirit. They die quietly, without any sign of defense. They are defenseless animals.

In the Old Testament, they were the only pure animals that God had accepted in sacrifice for forgiveness of sins. This is because of their innocent nature. Since they are clean and spotless animals, God temporarily accepted them for the purification of sin. When Adam and eve sinned, God covered their nudity by killing a clean lamb. He took the skin and covered their sins temporarily until he separated the goat-like from the lamb-like. This would not have been soif God had not provided a temporary forgiveness for them.

Only a lamb can temporarily cover human sin before God. Sheep are a group of lambs, not goats. They need a shepherd because they are defenseless. Sheep like to walk in groups. They are not individualistic. Any saint in a church who has an independent spirit is not a lamb and cannot be part of the sheep because sheep like to dwell together. They eat together and anything they are doing is in unity. This shows that they are one, and God loves unity, as long as it has a pure motive behind it. A true leader keeps God's people together, but a false leader disperses the sheep. To lead the flock, you must have a divine calling, or you will get confusion.

Sheep will not dwell in a pasture that does not have green grass. Neither will they dwell in a place without running water. Goats, on the other hand, will live any place, and eat anything and drink dirty water. We know that all of these descriptions are metaphoric descriptions because the pasture is a symbol of the church. The green grass is a symbol of the word of God. Which is the food for our souls. In other words, a true Christian will not stay in a church where there is no heavy teaching of the word of God or in a place where the Holy Spirit is not moving. The running water symbolizes the Holy Ghost. It is not remaining in one place. It moves in the lives of the true believers, producing life in their souls. Lamb-like people love the righteousness of God. Goat-like people love wickedness.

Lamb-like people do not gossip in the church. The goat-like people love gossiping. They cannot live without it. It is the energy for their souls. Lamb-like people love to be admonished for what they have done wrong. Goat-like people hate being corrected for their wrongdoings. They will defend themselves until death and may even kill for their own self-righteousness.

Every Christian is called to be lamb-like. We are called to put to death the Adamic nature, something we know we cannot go to heaven without undoing. It is our job to eliminate everything we know cannot save our lives.

A lamb always absorbs corrections and then changes. Goats will not tolerate correction. Therefore, they will run away and curse, even backslide. The goat-like people also claim to be Christians. It is not that they do not love God, but their nature prevents them from submitting themselves to the will of God. The will of God sometimes requires us to suffer unjustly. Goat-like people will not tolerate that. A goat-like person doesn't have the nature to tolerate suffering.

Judas Iscariot was a goat. That is why he betrayed Jesus. Cain was a goat. That is why he killed his own brother. Nimrod was also goat, and when he built the tower of Babel God caused the languages of men to be confused. Many others in the Bible were considered to be like goats because of their unrighteous nature.

So it is today. Many so-called Christians are considered as goats before God because of their reactions when they face problems and difficulties. Jesus, our example, suffered unjustly, yet he never complained or reacted badly in any circumstances (1 Peter 2:21). A lamb-like person becomes stronger through tribulations. Such people become wiser and maturer in God.

What makes a person a goat or a lamb? Again, it is their nature that differentiates them. Their spirits and attitudes reveal who they are, but you will never know that unless something crosses their paths, which make them reveal their true nature.

Goat-like people also act like lambs. They want you to believe that they are lambs. They will never accept that they indeed are goats. They will always have a way to justify their own way, but their nature reveals who they are. Spirit and attitude speaks louder than only words.

The real character of a lamb is a meek attitude. That was Jesus' nature. That is why John the Baptist called him the lamb of God that would take away the sins of the world. It takes a meek spirit to bear a burden unjustly. Goat-like people cannot bear any burden. They do not have the nature to do so. They may pretend they can, but when they get into the reality of it, when the burden becomes very heavy, they will react violently.

A goat's nature cannot be corrected. It will be very hard for a goat-like person to be saved. It will require the extended mercy of God, even though we know that the blood of Jesus is strong enough to change anyone's heart. It has to do with nature. They will not obey anything righteous. That is why God doesn't like goat-like people.

The main characteristic of sheep is that they do not drink in water that makes a lot of noise. They drink from quiet water. They know their master's voice and they will not follow strangers (John 10:7-16).

The Natural Life of Man Without Christ

Solomon said, in Ecc. 3:18, "I said in mine heart concerning the estate of the sons of men, that God might try them and that they might see that they themselves are beasts. As the beasts dieth, so is the sons of men. What befalleth one also befalleth the other. So man hath no preeminence above a beast; for all is vanity." A life without meaning is a worthless life. It was not God's plan for man to live like animals. It was because of Adam's sin that men find themselves in such a condition.

The Bible says, in Job 1:21, "naked I came out of my mother's womb and naked shall I return." Paul says in 1 Cor. 15:21, "the, first man is of the earth, he is earthly; the second is the Lord from Heaven. As is the earthly, such are they also that earthly: and is the heavenly, such are they also that are heavenly." Adam, the first man, was of the earth, so are his offspring. Jesus was of Heaven, and so are those who are born of spirit. What Adam had given us was a life of vanity, a life of misery, suffering, sickness and death at the end. But Jesus brought us life forever. Jesus asked what it would profit a man if he would gain the whole world and lose his soul. "All flesh is a grass and all the glory of man as the flower of the grass. The grass withereth and the flower thereof falleth away" (1Peter 1:24).

In all the beauty and the glory of man's life, God calls it vanity and the pursuit of the wind. Solomon himself was one of the greatest kings and one of the wisest men to ever live on the face of the earth. Yet he died with no hope, because he died in sin. Man's natural life is worthless without God. Our lives have no meaning if we don't have the substance of the eternal life in us.

Our lives are temporary. Our true hope is not here on this earth but in Heaven. Paul said that after he had gone through, if it's only for this life he would have hope, and he would be much more miserable than the beasts.

Natural man cannot comprehend the things of God. It takes the baptism of the Holy Spirit to open our eyes to understanding the things of God.

People today are able to make more and more inventions to confuse their brothers and sisters. Those who are more educated and skilled always tend to dominate the weakest ones. That is why Nimrod was able to build the Tower of Babel. He thought that he was smarter and wiser than the rest of the people.

God's purpose for our lives is much higher that we think. God gave us this life to repair the great damage that Adam did. It will take a period of six thousand years to restore man back to where he was created (GE. 1:26).

God's image was his spiritual virtue in Adam. He was the son of God on earth. God put his spirit in Adam to live above the flesh. Adam listened to his wife's voice and got carried away in the flesh and violated the law of life. He became the prisoner of the power of sin and death (Eph. 2:1-5). Adam was the one who sowed the corruptible seed into the human race.

Jesus had sowed the incorruptible seed of life into us and renewed our hopes to become the sons of God again. The natural beauties and the intellectual principals of the world are nothing more than vanity and dust before God. The natural knowledge of men cannot save a soul from death. There is no life in the natural productivity of men.

Holiness

Holiness should be the primary vision of every Christian, for the Bible says that without holiness no man shall see God. This means that whatever we may do in our Christian lives, if we don't live a holy life, everything we do will be in vain. People of the Body of Christ are called to be Christ-like people, a separated people, and people who strive to live holy before God. Holiness should not be in just one aspect but in all aspects of our lives.

We understand that there is a long process to be completely holy. Paul says in Eph. 4:24, "and that ye put on new man, which is created in righteousness and true holiness." After receiving the Holy Ghost's baptism, we are created in God's image in true holiness, which is the beginning of our lives in God. We must then walk in holiness daily. Holiness has a beginning and an end. The only way we can reach perfection in God is to walk in holiness everyday. We should be holy in our conversations, holy in our minds, holy in our sexual activities with our wives and holy behaviors with our children. This is our passport to eternal life.

The Bible says in 1 Cor. 3:17, "if any man defileth the temple of God, him shall God destroy; for the temple of God is holy, which temple ye are." We are the temples of God; we should be holy. If not, we are not the temples of God, because it should be holy.

God cannot dwell in filthy houses. If we are secretly living a filthy life when we claim to be Christians, then one day God will expose us into light, and we will die in our sins. We know that no one can be holy without the washing of the pure word of God. That is why it is required that holy minister brings the people in holiness. A filthy minister cannot produce a holy people, because what you are is what you will produce. Jesus said in Matt. 7:18-19, "a good tree will bring forth good fruit. A bad tree brings forth its bad fruit." So a good man of God will bring forth good people; a holy man of God can produce a holy people.

It is this way also for a man pretending to be a man of God when he is not. He will not and cannot produce a good people. "I beseech you therefore, brethren, by the mercies of God that ye present your bodies a living sacrifice, holy, and acceptable unto God which is your reasonable service. Not to be conformed to this world: But be ye transformed be the renewing of your mind, that ye may prove what is that good, and acceptable and perfect will of God" (Rom.12:1).

"Renewing of your mind" shows a process in holiness and a spiritual growth in God. I know that we cannot be holy in one day or even in a few years, but we have the mind to be holy, then we will put forth the effort, no matter what it may cost us. He then says not to be conformed to *this* world but transformed. By the renewing of your winds. What Paul really wanted to tell the roman Church was to stay away from the pleasures of the world. Of course we cannot be holy if we are participating in the worldly entertainment; if we are associating with people of the world, we cannot be holy. "The Lord is righteous in all his ways, holy in all his works" (Psalms 145:17). The Lord is holy; if he calls us, then we should be holy, as he is holy. For nothing unholy shall enter the third Heaven in holiest of holy where the throne of God is.

The Seven Destructive Ways Of The Flesh
(2 CORINTHIANS 11:13)

False Imaginations

The Bible says, in 2 Cor. 11:3, "I fear, lest by any means, as the serpent beguiled Eve through his subtlety, so your minds should be corrupted from the simplicity that is in Christ." False imaginations can corrupt your minds and cause great defeat in both your natural and spiritual life. When someone has an imaginary mind, he or she is always inventing things that are contrary to the Law of God. Imagination is one of the seven destructive ways. It is also the door that all the others will come through. When you have an imaginative mind, your life is like a city without a protective wall. Imagination is the key seducer of the whole human race. It was by false imagination that sin and death entered the world. Any inner voice that tells you to disobey the Law of God is one of the destructive ways of the flesh. Some imaginations can also come in a positive form, but the result of them may be very destructive. The only way your imaginations can be under control is if you receive the baptism of the Holy Ghost and walk by the spirit. You must not obey the negative ways of the flesh.

Pride

Pride is one of the most incurable diseases someone can have in his or her life. When you are proud, you can only see with one eye. As you know, it requires two eyes in very good spiritual condition to walk in the path of righteousness. It is said, in Prov.6.16 that God hates people with a proud look. Proud people can easily become ignorant by thinking that they know everything. Proud people often live a miserable life. They are intolerant, and their spirit is very narrow-minded. None of them ever does anything right. They never admit their mistakes in anything, and they are narrow-minded. Pride is a big infirmity that can paralyze any person, in institutions both religious and social, in the church, government and society. It will be very difficult for any of these institutions to grow because pride itself is a barrier.

In the day we are living in, in most religious denominations most of the leaders of the church are very proud of their achievements and their academic knowledge. They glorify themselves for every single accomplishment. They will never accomplish anything spiritual because of their nature. Most of the time those proud individuals are also liars. When they make mistakes, they refuse to be corrected. They may have problems and they will not seek for help. They will let you know how well they are doing when everything is falling apart. If you marry a proud person, you may be very miserable for the rest of your life. Proud people can be hypocrites. Most of the time, they boast about things they give to someone. Even though they might be in danger, they will pretend that everything is in control. If someone offers to help them, they will automatically try to get rid of him of her (Psalms 101:5).

Hatred

It is said, in 1 John 2:11, "he that hates his brother is in darkness, and walks in darkness, and know not where he goeth, because that darkness hath blinded his eyes." People who have hatred in their hearts can be miserable in all aspects of their lives. Hatred can also create bitterness and animosity. Animosity is the source of all kinds of financial hardship and difficulties in human life. It can also create sadness, loneliness and even incurable diseases.

The Bible says Christians should not go to bed with any bitterness and anger in their hearts. Actually some Christians don't consider hatred as a sin; they can keep it in their hearts as long as they wish and think it's nothing. The Bible says all the law is fulfilled in one phrase, "thou shall love thy neighbor as thyself." Divine love has no hypocrisy and we can not be unrighteous and expect to go to Heaven. If we keep animosities in our hearts, the Holy Ghost cannot have full control of our minds and subconscious minds. If you are still in darkness, then you are not completely free to become a new creature in Christ.

Paul says, in Gal.5:15 "but if ye bite and devour one another, take heed that ye be not consumed one of another." After that he gave a list of things that Christians should not do. In verse 22 he listed many things true Christians should practice.

Understand that hatred is like a nail in the middle of our spiritual hearts. If we keep hatred in our hearts, we cannot go further in God. First, we will become spiritually paralyzed. Then, we will never grow up. Finally, we cannot produce any good fruit, which would allow us to become spiritually mature in God.

After a certain time, God will reject us, and we will find ourselves back in the world, doing things even the ungodly people would not do.

Paul says, in Eph. 6:11, to put on all of God's armor so that you will be able to stand firm against all strategies and tricks of the devil. Many preachers may view rulers of this dark world as a physical devil, but the word *ruler* describes wicked spirits that ruled the human race. Notice verse 12 says, "for we are not fighting against people made of flesh and blood but against the evil rulers and authorities of the unseen world, against those mighty powers of darkness who rule this world and against wicked spirits in high places." What Paul referred to here was the Pharisees' and the Saducces' religious systems. We all know what they did to Jesus, the savior of the world.

Those men were highly religious and very wicked. They occupied high positions in the system, but no one was able to judge them except God. We know what God did with them in 70 A.D. so if we are not careful, the same thing can happen to us of the twentieth century also. God will judge us, and we will be destroyed in the great battle of Armageddon. We must double our efforts to love our brothers in the Lord and even those in the world.

If Christians have hatred in their hearts, then they will not be able to save others in this wicked world. It requires a lot of charity to help save people in the world, especially the ones who are not in Christ. Charity is not proud or rude. Those who have their faith established in Christ must also become models, not only for those in the church but also for those in the world.

Adultery

This is one of the most powerful tools the devil is using to destroy many great men of God, great saints who loved God so much and made many great sacrifices for God's people (James 1:13-14). Let no man say when he is tempted, "I am tempted of God." For God cannot be tempted with evil, neither tempteth He any man. Every man is tempted, when he enticed and is drawn away of his own lust. Temptation comes from the lure of our own evil desires. Verse 15 says, "when lust hath conceived it bringeth forth sin; and sin when it is finished bright forth death."

Women in a sense are one of the greatest challenges man faces in serving God faithfully. Woman is a great companion that God gave to man. At the same time, woman can be the main problem that man has to deal with in saving his soul. Since woman was created with a man's rib, it became a profound mystery between man and woman. Naturally, men love beautiful women, and women love good-looking men.

Men and women have a bond that enables them to control themselves. Christians should try to maintain a high moral standard that can please God. It is said, in Genesis 6:2-3, "the sons of God saw the daughters of men that they were fair; and they took them wives, of all which they chose. Then the lord said, my spirit shall not always dwell in man for that he also is flesh: yet his days shall be an hundred and twenty years." This chapter shows us there's a natural affection in men for women. That natural affection causes men to become blind on spiritual things of God.

It is said, in Gen. 6:12, "God looked upon the earth and behold, it was corrupted." When men from the righteous line chose to marry women of the unrighteous, then God reduced the days of men on the earth. God replies,"man is nothing but flesh and my spirit shall not dwell in man."

Men would rather sacrifice everything for women, so God regretted that he created man. Some men consider women as their idols. They worship women more than they worship God the Creator. You would not believe what a man would do to have a woman he loves. It would go beyond your imagination. Men will lie and will even abandon their own parents for a woman. When they are in love with a woman, they become their defenders and protectors.

If one woman is not enough for him, he will go out looking for extramarital affairs. Some men are never satisfied with one woman. They try to conquer every beautiful woman they can. Many men find their glory in women. Man feels very important when he has a beautiful woman as his wife. What kind of spirit is that? Where does it come from?

God is holy, and he wants man to be holy as He is. Paul says, in Gal.5:13 "ye have been called unto the liberty but let not your liberty become an occasion to live after the flesh." Natural men live by instincts, just like the beasts live by instincts. It's a spirit that is in every man. Even though we were created in God's image, we still do wrong. We must try to control our desires and instincts (Romans. 7:8).

Paul had discovered the law of sin and death in man and the law of the spirit of life in Jesus Christ. He was able to differentiate these two laws and decided which one he should obey. In verse 22, he says that there's one thing he does: "for I delight in the law of God after the inward man." It is said, in verse 18, "for I know that in me that is in my flesh dwelleth no good for to will is present with me; but how to perform that which is good I find not." We cannot rely on our own natural strength to control our carnal mind. We must rely on God and in his mercy to help us in our infirmities. If we rely on ourselves, the flesh will deceive us.

Naturally there's nothing spiritual that dwells in man. That is the reason why we cannot trust ourselves. As Christians, we must stand still and never bow down our knees before the flesh. In Matthew 4:8-9, the devil asked Jesus to bow down his knees before him and promised to give Him all the glories of the world if he did. If the devil had asked Jesus the Son of God to bow down, what about us? Humans are one hundred percent flesh and blood. Jesus was fifty percent human and fifty percent spirit, but he had all the natural instincts, just like us. Jesus had natural appetites but he never obeyed the devil. He showed us that we could become one hundred percent spiritual, but we must learn how to balance our Adamic natures. When adultery comes to your mind, you need not to obey the voice of the flesh. Ask yourself what the consequences will be after the act. If the answer is important for your spiritual life, then you should not do it.

The devil uses our emotions to make us commit these sins. The devil can put us on a high mountain by using our emotions to show us the beauty of the flesh and its pleasures if we are not spiritually awake. Note that Jesus had rebuked the desire, which was questioning his authority. He automatically knew that those kinds of desires were not of God but of the devil.

I believe that every Christian should do the same. When you face a temptation in your life, you should stop for a minute and begin to respond within yourself. If it is the devil's trap, don't do it. Most of the time, we are tempted by the devil, but we must be able to stand still and pass all our tests without fail. If we do pass all our tests, then God will put us a step higher, spiritually. If we fail our tests, we will not grow spiritually. "For ye were sometimes in darkness, but now ye are light in the Lord: walk as children of light" (Eph. 5:8-9).

It is said, in verse 11, "have no fellowship with the unfruitful works of darkness, but rather reprove them, for it is a shame even to speak of those things which are done in secret." You know that anytime you have a relationship with someone who is not your wife or husband, you take part in the dark work of the flesh. Therefore, you are in communion with the devil. The devil is also using your body as a vessel of uncleanness. Christians should never commit adultery! If one day you find yourself in that situation, you must quickly repent and ask God for forgiveness. Then you must also ask your partner to forgive you, so you can be completely delivered. If not, your conscience will never be truly clear, no matter what position you may occupy in the church. Every Christian should be able to maintain a high moral standard. Indeed, we should strive to keep our personal holiness together. Some people are able to keep themselves from falling in adultery, but some cannot. If we call ourselves Christians, then we should do better than the others of the world. It is not very easy to live in such a corrupt world and keep ourselves holy.

Our Lord Jesus asks us to pray! If you carefully watch yourself, you will not fall into the devil's traps. Jesus knew that without the Holy Ghost it would be very hard to stay spiritually awake but we must. This is the reason why God gave us the Holy Spirit, so we could keep ourselves holy from the filth of this world. Personal holiness should be our main goal, and we should fight to maintain it "Therefore, if a man purges himself from this, he shall be a vessel unto honor sanctified to meet the master's requirements to prefer unto every good work" (Col. 3:15) (2 Tim. 2:21).

Love of Money

The Bible says, in 1 Tim. 6:10, that the love of money is the root of all evil. Some people craved money, wandered from the faith and pierced themselves with many sorrows.

We have three forces that rule the world: sex, money and power. People will do anything to have them. The Bible says, in 1 John 1:16-17, that we should not love the world and things of the world, for what is in the world is the lust of the flesh, lust of the eye and the pride of life. It is said, in verse 17, "the world passed with the things in it but the word of God shall endure forever." If we love the world so much, the love of the father is not in us.

When we take a look into man's life, he is spending all his time looking for money. We work several hours a day to gain money in the world, so we should seek God the same way.

Without good health, we cannot reach others in the world. For Christians good health is better than money. God is the one who gives health and natural prosperity to men. If God had acted only like us, none of us would be alive today. I know that some people are filthy rich, yet are miserable. Why? Because they don't have God in their lives. Some of them are very sick in their bodies and they cannot be cured. If they could give away all their money just to have good health, they would do it. Their money cannot buy them health, so they die with their money. We need to think twice before loving money more than loving God our creator. Money is good to have but it must not become our gods.

There's only one true eternal God, the Creator of the universe. The Bible says that there are no other gods besides Him. He is the only true God! Money should not dominate our lives because it is not our god. It's only a true servant! We can only use money while we are living here on earth (1 Tim.6:9). Paul says those who are rich fall into temptations and the traps of the devil. He says that they will have all kinds of foolish desires that will lead them into destruction.

Christians should not only use their money for their personal belongings but also for the Lord. When we say not to love money, that does not mean to throw away your money. We will not let money become a god for us. Anything that becomes our god will dominate our lives. Then we become its slaves. The Bible says not to become anyone's slave but God is your Creator. The whole human race becomes slaves of money. They seek money more than they seek God.

The Bible says, in Rom. 1:21, "when they knew God neither were thankful, became vain in their imagination and their foolish heart was darkened." Many Christians become blind by the care of this life. They keep themselves constantly busy in the things of the world. Then they become slaves of the world. Some do not even have time to attend services anymore. Why, Because they are always working and never have time for their soul.

The devil keeps them in bondage until they die and lose their souls. The Bible asks what it would profit a man if he would gain the whole world and lose his soul! That's why we must be spiritually awake and we need to keep our spiritual eyes open and our spiritual senses fully developed, so we do not fall into the devil traps.

The best way the devil can trap us is with money. Christians should not love it too much because of its danger. When we love money too much, we will forsake our God and we do not want to do that. The Bible says, in Mat. 6:33-34, "seek ye first the kingdom of God, and His righteousness; and all these things shall be added unto you." It is said, in verse 34, "take no thought for the morrow. So, for the morrow shall take care itself. Sufficient unto the day is the evil there for." Christians who care too much for the perishable things of the world will never spiritually stand on their feet, because their minds are occupied with things of this world. After awhile, these people have always become those that create troubles in church. They never take a stand on anything, spiritually speaking. So when they see that someone who is truly seeking God with all of his or her heart get blessed, they become jealous. If we do not give ourselves completely to the things of God, we preoccupy our minds with the vanity of this world.

Disobedience

In Rom. 5:19 Paul says, "for as by one man's disobedience, many were made sinners, so by the obedience of one, shall many be made righteous." Brothers and sisters, disobedience is something that all Christian should watch carefully in their lives. People with a little disobedience in their lives cannot be saved. The greatest problem God has with man is that man has a rebellious nature. It was an act of disobedience that caused all the sickness and difficulties that we are facing today. If Adam did not disobey the laws of God, you and I would not be living in the condition that we are living in now.

In Eph. 2:2 Paul mentioned a group of people that God called "children of disobedience," and there is a spirit in them. That spirit represents a supernatural force that motivates them to act a certain way. It causes them to live in ignorance. Paul says that we were among those who were predestined to perish, but God in his great mercy loves us and calls us out to become partakers of his nature. When you have a disobedient nature, this could cause you to rebel against the will of God without even realizing it. People sometimes say that if they do not understand something, they will not even obey it. It's different in the kingdom of God. God says a sacrifice without obedience is worthless. You can make all kinds of sacrifices, but if you have a rebellious heart it's all in vain. Samuel said, "hath the Lord as great delight in burnt offerings and sacrifices, as in obeying the voice of the Lord" (1 Sam. 15:22). Behold in verse 23, "for rebellion is as the sin of witchcraft, and stubbornness is as iniquity and idolatry."

God hates rebellious people, and because of this He nearly destroyed the whole nation of Israel. The Pharisees had a rebellious attitude toward Jesus' preaching.

They conspired to kill him, and they did. In A.D. 70 Jesus came in vengeance. All the roots of the Pharisees and the Sadducees system were destroyed forever.

We don't need any signs of rebellion remaining in our lives. We must get rid of all disobedience. We may repent and find

God's favor, but that does not mean He will not forget our disobedience. If it arises again then we will be punished from the very first one to the last; it will be the greatest punishment.

Many people think that they can disobey God and then later repent. It is true that God is a God of mercy, but at the same time he keeps record of our sins. The only way God will forget our sins is by true repentance. And even after our repentance we must make a commitment not to sin again. If we do in ignorance, we may again find his forgiveness, but if we intentionally keep doing it, we will face his punishment. A little disobedience had caused even Moses, father of the nation of Israel, to miss the enjoyments of the Promised Land. He ignorantly hit the rock, instead of speaking to the rock, to get the water to come out. The people caused him to lose his temper, and he forgot whom he was dealing with. He made the greatest mistake of his life.

Envy

Prov. 24:1 says, "be not thou envious against evil men, neither desire to be with them. For their heart studieth destruction and their lips talk of mischief." Envy is also incurable disease that we should not allow to enter our hearts, because once it gets there it will bring forth bad fruits and many other destructive and evil habits that will conquer our souls. When people is an envious person, they will automatically become jealous, and they will become hypocrites, just like the Pharisees. They were very religious and very malicious hypocrites. Jesus called them "white tombs." We do not want to be like white tombs, where we look very nice on the outside but are filthy on the inside. What could cause someone to become envious? Envy is one of the 133 works of the flesh and what brings it into the heart of a saint is when he doesn't have enough love in his heart for his fellow brothers and sisters. The root of bitterness begins to grow.

Envy doesn't come by itself, there must be something there that causes it to grow. When someone has an envious heart, there is a possibility for that person to become a murderer! (Gal. 5:21).

That spirit is in the heart of many saints in the church of the body of Christ and even in some pastors (James 4:5). James says, in James 4:7, "submit yourselves therefor to God.

Resist the devil and he will flee from you. Draw nigh to God and he will draw nigh to you. Cleanse your hands, ye sinners; and purify your hearts, ye double minded."

God doesn't call us to become double minded. The only thing we should have in our hearts is love. Nothing evil should dwell in our hearts because once it gets there, it will call on all the others to come in. Then shortly unclean spirits will invade our whole soul. Jealousy is the twin of envy. They are brother and sister. When one of them gets in, it will call on its twin, first and after that all the family will join in, all 133 of them. All of them will get into your heart and you will become the devil in the flesh.

Love

Paul says, "though I speak with the tongues of men and angels, and have not charity, I am become as sounding brass or a tinkling cymbal. Though I have the gift of prophecy, and understand all mysteries and all knowledge; and though I have all faith so that I could remove mountains, and have not charity, I have nothing" (1 Cor. 13:1-2). Charity is divine love! Some Christians today do not even know the true meaning of the word charity. Some think it is when you give away your goods or money to those in need. In Verse 3 Paul says, "though I bestow all my goods to feed the poor and though I give even my body to be burned, if I have not charity it profith me nothing" (Eph. 5:2).

Walk in love, as Christ also hath loved us, and hath given Himself for us an offering and a sacrifice to God for a sweet smelling savour. Jesus' love and obedience to God was like a sweet savour. How do our attitudes, jealousies and bitterness smell to God today? If we call ourselves Christians and we have no love for one another, we are not what we claim to be. The word Christian means Christ-like. We have to walk in His footsteps. Jesus had love in His heart for us. He laid down His life for us; we must do the same for our brothers and sisters in Christ, and even for the others in the world. We must love them and show love to them. If not, we cannot save them.

Verse 4 in 1 Cor. 13 shows us what charity is. It says, "charity is long suffereth, kind, charity envieth not. It does not flaunt itself; it is not puffed up; not behaving itself unseemingly; seek not her own interest, is not easily provoked, thinking no evil rejoiceth not iniquity. Rejoice only in the truth. These are the fruits of charity!" Christians should do their best to measure up to these things.

We cannot simply claim we have love without proving it (John 13:1-15).

Jesus demonstrated his love to his Disciples by washing their feet, and he asked them to do the same for their fellow man. It was an allegory to prove His everlasting love to them (John 13:34). Jesus said it is a commandment to love one another. It is a must. This means that everything we claim we are doing for God, we are doing in vain if we don't first love our brothers and sisters in Christ.

People can have all kinds of religious manifestations, but everything they do is to please themselves and to protect their personal interests. We must reach a point where we can lay down these things to pick up the spiritual attributes of God. The principal law of the church of God is that every single member of the church must love each other without any reserve. Our spiritual growth is deeply dependent upon that. God's plans for the earth are to build an everlasting kingdom; a kingdom different from all the other kingdoms that previously existed. This kingdom will be built with pure love.

There are three kinds of love. There is the divine love that comes from above. It is a love without interest. It is the love that comes from the God of love. He is invisible, immortal, and God is the Supreme Chief above all. He is the only true God, the father of our Lord and savior Jesus Christ.

The next kind of love is the intimate love a husband has for his wife or a wife has for her husband. That is why a man leaves his family, to become one with his wife. It is because of the loving relationship they have between one another.

The last love is familial love. This is the love a parent has for his child. This is the kind of love beasts also have for their offspring. This is what we call natural love.

In this kind of love there is a natural protection provided by the parents, from the first generation to the last.

We understand that each of these loves has their fruits. Divine love produces eternal life! It was divine love that caused God to send His only begotten son to die on the cross for you and me. It was also divine love that caused Jesus to obey his father and come down to save the whole human race from the sins of Adam. That was the fruit of divine love manifested for you and me. The fruit of intimate love is the children and the grandchildren. When a man and a woman fall in love, they will produce fruit a few years later. Their fruit is visible. All eyes can definitely see what this kind of love can produce. The fruit of natural love is the kind of protection provided by the parents for their children. The children will feel secure under the wings of their parents. The spirits, attitudes, and behaviors, moral or immoral, reflected in a child represent the fruit of their parents! God calls us to raise our children according to His law. The love they have for their children causes them to provide a protection that reflects who they are and what they believe. We know that it is not every parent that loves his or her child. Some parents are not even worthy to be called parents. They do not know what it takes to be a parent. Some parents put shameful things in their children. Some parents raise their children to become trouble for society. Did you know that it is a lack of love from the parents? They did not do a good job in their children, and this is because they did not find love for themselves. So, they have nothing to give to their children and this can go on for generations.

True Worshipping

Worshipping is one the most important elements in a Christian's spiritual life. There are three kinds of worshipping:

1. True Worshipping
2. False Worshipping
3. Ignorant Worshipping

A Christian heart must be pure before God so he can accept his worshipping (John 4:20-24). Before people come to church, they must prepare their minds at home, in order to start worshipping. They must have the right disposition when they come to church and the right attitudes. Before someone comes to worship God, he or she must truly believe that God exists. They must have his or her faith rooted in God. The word *worshipping* means giving a high honor to a higher authority. *Proskuneo* is the Greek word for worship, humbleness or kissing a hand on your knees. The key factor in worshipping is the motif of your heart (Exodus 30:34-38). God wanted Moses to differentiate Him from any other god that seemed to exist (John 12:1-3). A humble spirit, this is the attitude that Christians should have before God. The woman's hair symbolized her glory, but she dried Jesus' feet with her hair (Exodus 20:1).

There is a divine order that must be executed before starting worshipping in the church! The order is that the pastor must begin first and then the people will follow (Num. 2:2). There must be a group of holy men in charge of the worship services (Peter 2:5).

After Jesus cleans and purifies us then He expects us to give all ourselves to become true living sacrifices to Him, the odors of our lives must please him. If not, we can become depraved minded Christians. We cannot worship God in our own ways, but we can only worship him the way he wants us to worship him (Matt. 15:1-9).

The Pharisees invented their own ways to worship God, and God was not pleased with that. That is one of the reasons he had judged them in A.D. 70 in the great destruction of Jerusalem. Then we also find Christians who are worshipping God correctly but with the wrong motives (Mal. 1:6-14). In everything God has a specific way to present or offer something to him. If we do not follow the guidelines first, then we will miss the blessings that He has for us (1 Sam. 13:8-14) (Matt. 23:23-28). The ignorant worshippers are those who worship God in mystery. They do not have the proper knowledge of the word of God, so they worship a god by building in their minds a mental image of someone with a long beard sitting on a throne. They materialize God in their minds, and that is what they worship. That is wrong! (John 4:22) (Gal. 4:8) (Rom. 1:22-23) When God gave the Ten Commandments to Moses, he told him not to let the people worship a god by building a mental picture, portraying someone in their minds. They should not believe that this is the way to worship him as their God. False worshippers are those who worship God by appearances. They do not serve God in the simplicity of the heart but in exhibitions to be great in the eyes of men (Matt. 23:27).

The Pharisees were the formalists that worked in simulations and appearances (Luke 18:10-14). The true worshippers are those who worship God in spirit and the truth. They worship God in faith. This means that they do not build mental pictures in their minds of a being to worship. They know that God is a spirit and therefore cannot be worshipped by visual images.

Abel was the first man who had worshipped God in faith (Heb. 11:4)). Cain, on the other hand, was an ignorant worshipper! He did not have enough faith in himself to trust God like Abel did. He became jealous and killed his brother. The true worshippers worship God in the name of Jesus, which means that they worship him with the understanding of the truth (Coloss. 3:18) (Eph. 5:20).

The Mystery of the Ungodliness

This is one of the most profound and complex subjects, and it is not easy to understand! People always think that the mystery of the ungodliness is something they can only see in the ungodly world. However, the reality is that the mystery of the ungodliness is more likely to be seen in the lives of those so-called Christians or the followers of Christ.

Some people think that when they go to church, pay their tithes, study their Bibles and do not commit adultery, that this is all they need to do. They are in the perfect will of God. They are pure, holy and if they die they next day, they will go to Heaven and be in the bride of Christ. What we actually see is the contrary. In fact, most of these so-called Christians do not really understand the concept of Christianity. They do not really know what it takes to become a true, dedicated Christian or follower of Christ. The mystery of it is that these people could even be in position of leadership, teaching people, when they need to learn the right ways and the true principles of God themselves. Most of them are so proud that they will not submit their lives to the true divine principles of God to become the true Disciples of Christ. Some of them have the skills and the abilities to speak. They learn how to mix their own imaginations with the word of God. They arrange their ideas around the words of God and present them to the people, those who are sleeping and were predestined to perish, who will listen to them and follow them. What they do not know is that these men are the instruments of Satan sent to deceive those who were predestined to perish.

Today there are many goat-like people, who present themselves to the people as lamb-like. There are many wolves claiming that they are shepherds, but the day is coming where God will reveal their true identities, and everyone shall see who they really are. Paul says, in 2 Cor. 11:3, "as the serpent beguilt Eve by its subtleties, I fear that your mind be corrupt by the simplicity which is in Christ." The simplicity that was in Christ caused the Pharisee to believe that He was not the Son of God. They were so high in their imaginations and so proud that they thought Jesus was too lowly to be anything in the kingdom of God, under the law. He came among them as a weak plant. There was nothing in him to attract them. There was nothing that would cause them to believe that He was indeed the Son of God. This was the mystery of the ungodliness! The reason why it was so for them was because they were not real. They had only a form of righteousness. There was nothing real in what they were doing.

What we see today is the same thing! Many claim to be the followers of Christ but when you examine their lives closely, you see nothing in them that would match what they say. Most of them are spiritually infirm. Their lives were spiritually paralyzed. The Bible says that no man can fool God! If we are not real, God knows and you can bet that one day His judgment will come on us, just as it had for the false Jewish religious system in A.D. 70 God destroyed them from the root to the top.

Spiritual infirmities are our primary enemies. This is something that we must watch diligently. These things could cause us to become so spiritually blinded that it would be impossible to see or understand the things of God because when we are spiritually blind, it is possible to become depraved minded.

When someone has a depraved mind he or she will become corrupted! When we become corrupted we will be subjected to undergo the judgment of God.

I believe that the greatest mystery today is the mystery of the ungodliness! This mystery is so deep it's almost impossible for us to understand it without a special touch from God. Men of our time are so spiritually blinded and ignorant of the things of God that we ask ourselves how they could possibly make it to the new earth. We can see how the mystery of the ungodliness works in the religious world, how it works in the natural world and how it works even in the true Church of the Body Christ. It can be seen in the leaders and those so-called Christians.

In Eph. 6:11, Paul shows us our spiritual warfare, telling us to put on the armor of God, that we may stand against the wiles of the devil. In verse 12 he says, "for we do not wrestle against flesh and blood, but against the rulers of the darkness of this world, against spiritual wickedness in high places."

Paul shows us five principal forces that we have to fight against, and we must overcome all of them in order to reach full spiritual maturity. Preachers sermonize these forces as separate beings from somewhere in space that came down to earth to persecute and torment the human race. The fact is that these forces dwell in men's and women's lives on this earth, not from somewhere else. Wicked spirits that are part of the human nature. We must overcome the spirit of principalities in our lives. Those that have that spirit always want to rule over people. The spirit of darkness that dwells in the human world is the spirit that came from Adam, our father. He created a world of darkness when he fell from the spiritual condition in which he was created. It is a spirit that is resisting the will of God. Their attitude is to live according to the vanity of this world, and these spirits are powerful. They can keep people captive. The can cause people to become slaves of the flesh. They can cause them to dwell in spiritual blindness. They produce a total of 133 works of the flesh that can dominate our lives in a way that can bond us to the law of sin and death.

What we call principalities are the powers that rule the human life and cause them to live for themselves, away from God, the father of all creation. As I have said at the beginning of this subject, these spirits not only dwell in the people of the ungodly world, but more likely manifest in the church.

Spiritual wickedness in high places also describes the churches of the Body of Christ and other churches of the religious world! Some leaders and some Christians of the churches never change their nature and at the same time are very religious. When you know the truth of the word of God and are never willing to put it into practice in your life, you will become a wicked force that is working contrary to the will of God and against the true saints of the Body of Christ. This is also what we call the mystery of ungodliness, because all of these people are in the church. If someone didn't know any better, they could get trapped and bound by their works, just as the false church we call religious Babylon. They too thought that they were doing the will of God. Many people believe in them and would even destroy innocent lives for the sake of the system. This is what took place in the past and most of us knew it. That is the spirit of error in operation and many get trapped in that false religious system. Did you know that the greatest mystery today is the mystery of the ungodliness? These five supernatural forces are a part of the Adamic nature, and if we are not careful, they can carry us to our graves with no hope of a resurrection! That is why we must be sincere and honest with ourselves. Otherwise we will be like the man that beat the wind; our lives will not have any purpose even though we might spend all our lives in church. All we have done could have been in vain. Jesus said, in Matt 7:24-27, "whosoever hear my words and put them not in practice, are like a man who built his house on sand and when strong winds come and beat that house, it fell because it was built on sand. But those who heareth my words and put them in practice are like wise men who built their houses on the solid rocks and when the strong winds beat against that house, it stood because it had been built on solid rock."

Spiritual infirmities are the enemies that we are fighting against. They are our hidden enemies, because we know that if we are not careful, they can destroy our souls. When we know where our true enemies are located, then we can have a plan to learn how to destroy them. The mystery of it is that most Christians do not know what their enemies are. They are looking for a different being called Satan or the Devil, when their true enemies are within. Anytime you have a desire that is contrary to the will of God; you should not fulfill it. Did you know that the Adamic nature could become more wicked even after conversion, if it is not wisely cultivated?

We must give ourselves one hundred percent, without any compromises. When the devil tempted Jesus, He made no compromises with that desire. He immediately identified it for what it was and automatically rebuked the desire. That desire was Jesus' hidden enemy and he knew it. He identified His enemy, fired back and destroyed that desire. In Prov. 6:14-19, we find six hidden enemies that dwell in men.

God says that He hates these things and one he holds in abomination. He hates anyone who has these kinds of spirits dwelling in them! A person that has a proud look, a lying tongue, hands that shed innocent blood, hearts that devise wicked imaginations, feet that are swift in running to mischief, a false witness that speaks lies and he that sows discord among brethren; these are our hidden enemies! If God hated them, we must hate them too. Jer. 17:9 mentions that the heart of men is deceitful and above all things, desperately wicked. Who can know this? Gal. 5:16-22 mentions the fruit of the flesh and the fruit of the spirit. We must choose, just as Adam had to choose, either life or death.

The devil is playing games with many people in the church today. When I say devil, I mean the spirits of the flesh, which keep many people captive. They are falling into a deep sleep, so they cannot become truly spiritual. When you remain spiritually blind, and you are in the church, the devil can use you to persecute the real saints of God. The reason is because your soul is still attached to your body, and all of the animal instincts influence the spirit and the soul because their subconscious minds have never been renewed.

Many people who have been around the church for so long, put on a form of righteousness. The may walk like it, talk like it, move like it, dress like it and all they have done is for nothing more than appearances to fool people. Some preachers may have their heads filled with knowledge of the word of God. They learn how to repeat it with high skill, and they develop a spirit of supremacy over the people. They are Adamically prepared and well educated, but the word of God is never put into practice in their lives. These are the kinds of men that always fall into corruption, because they don't have enough substance to fight against the spirit of the flesh. The mystery of it is that when they fall into a sinful and corrupt condition, they will not stop preaching! They will do their best to justify themselves to prove that there is nothing wrong with them. It is people that don't like them that are trying to destroy their ministry. Rom. 1:18 says the wrath of God is revealed from Heaven against all ungodliness and unrighteousness of men who hold the truth captive. Many may portray this to the religious world but there are many people in the church of the Body of Christ that kept the truth of the word of God captive! They know their weaknesses but they never been willing to work on them, and they will not allow the word of God to purify their sins. These are the people who become wise in their own eyes, and they will always see other people's problems without realizing their own. Most people who are spiritually infirm never realize that they are. God always has problems with these types of people.

The Adamic nature is one of the most mysterious things that we cannot comprehend with our natural abilities. That is the reason why God compared it to a serpent, because it is very mysterious and subtle. We naturally know that a serpent is a very mystic animal! It is simply metaphoric language that portrays man's Adamic nature. We know that the Adamic nature is very subtle, even after conversion.

The Adamic nature of man can also learn how to become religious and never change! That is why you can see many men in the religious world and even in the true body of Christ preach great things, even the mysteries of the God head, and never change their nature. Yet, when they stand up to preach, you can easily say this is a true man of God. This is the mystery of the ungodliness. Yes, it is just to see how far the Adamic nature can go, even in the holy things of God. People preach things, but when you follow their personal lives, you don't see anything that reflects what they preach. In what they preach and how they live their private lives, day and night, you cannot see anything to match what they are preaching. That is the mystery of the ungodliness! A preacher should live what he preaches! When people look back into your life, they should see a clear reflection of what you preach, with no problem. If you preach Christ, they should be able to see Christ in you life and nothing more. If you preach holiness, they should see holiness reflected greatly in your life and this is how it should be! How can the people have confidence in a preacher if he tells them not to do something and he is doing it secretly? A pastor's life should be like an open book that everyone should be able to read clearly and without any doubts.

Your life should be like a mirror that reflects Christ to the people. They should not find anything indecent or ugly to blame you for. You must be an example for the people in all things. That is why if someone feels that he or she cannot keep to a high standard, he or she should not get involved in the field of pastoring people. That is why Jesus called the Pharisees "white tombs" that look good on the outside, but smell very bad on the inside. It is because He knew that they were not real.

Grace and Suffering

Leaders of the religious world teach that we are in the dispensation of grace and that they can do whatever they want, even though they may intentionally sin against the law of God. The word grace means favor. It means that we were not worthy of it, that is why it's called favor.

In Esther 2:17, the king was a type of Christ. It was because of disobedience that the king had rejected Queen Vashti. Esther had found favor in the king's eyes. As we all know, Queen Vashti was typical of the nation of Israel and Esther was typical of the Gentile nations, which had found grace in Jesus' sight.

The grace of God gave us a period of two thousand years in which we can prepare ourselves to become the bride of Christ (Gen. 32:3-5) (Gen. 39:1-4). To find God's favor you must be faithful! There can never be favor without faithfulness (Ruth 2:1-13) (Gen. 2:7). when God put Adam and Eve in the Garden of Eden, they had found the favor of God. The Garden of Eden was a metaphor of the church (Rom. 5:12) (2 Chron. 20:20) (Gen. 3:21). The covering was a type of the grace of God. It was a type of and a righteous foundation for the posterity. After grace, suffering always follows (1 Peter 4:1) (Rom. 8:17-18). To become heirs of Christ, we must go through trials and tribulations. The point is that we must keep a good spirit in the midst of it all. Sometimes the perfect will of God is manifested by many trials and tribulations. Jesus was our example. Paul the apostle was also an example! (2 Cor. 11:23-28).

It is true that the grace of God was offered to the human race without any exception, but we must qualify ourselves to God after we find his grace.

If we have found his grace and we remain in our sinful ways, thinking that we are in God's grace, then we are fooling ourselves. Remember grace is a favor. We must be obedient. We must first repent our sins and accept Christ in our lives as our Savior.

In God's grace there are also requirements. After we find God's grace, we must practice personal holiness. This is the first key! Then we must walk in perseverance. We must be willing to put into practice, the word of God. We must love our brothers and sisters in faith. We must govern our natural families correctly, in total obedience of the word of God. After these requirements are met, then God is willing to add us into his spiritual family on the earth. He will then baptize us with his Holy Spirit and we will become a part of what God is doing in this present age.

In the religious world, many are walking in complete ignorance! They claim that the grace of God is eternal security. They believe they can do many evil things intentionally, then claim that God is a God of mercy and that the blood of Jesus will clean them again, of their intentional sins. No one can take the grace of God for granted and think they can get away with it. God will not leave intentional sins unpunished!

After someone has received the baptism of the Holy Spirit, God forgets all of their past sins. He or she now has a brand new start, but now all intentional sins are recorded in the memory of God. Ignorant sins can still be forgiven, but not intentional sins. When the Bible says, "if we sin, we have lawyer in Heaven," this is not for intentional sins but ignorant ones. Many take the grace of God for granted. That is why Jesus says, in Matt. 7:21-24, "many will say to me on that day, Lord have we not done all these great things in your name?" Then Jesus says He will openly tell them to "depart from me. I knew you not. You that work in iniquity." We cannot have a disordered lifestyle and think that we are in the perfect will of God.

About the Author

My name is Fritz Bazin; I am an associate pastor of South Florida Assembly of the Body of Christ. I have a thirst for learning, in seventeen years I have studied a variety of subjects, and different biblical fields, including Theology.

My professional career of thirteen years as the assistant Director of the puchasing Department at Turnberry Isle Resort and Club.

I am also married with three children: Two boys and a girl.

My goal as a minister is someday to be able to minister to the world by establishing a worldwide ministry. A ministry with a different vision, different ways to reach lost souls for the Lord and Savior Jesus Christ.

My first book is Chazowth 2000.

I've received many offers from different publishers all over the country willing to publish the work, but I want to publish with 1st Books Library because of the kind of work that they do and the kind of service they offer.

I've also received many letters from different publishers all over the world that have read the work, and evaluated it as one of the most powerful and provocative piece of documents ever put together in this century.

Please, when that book is published, buy a copy.
As for this book, "The Enemies of the Human Soul," please buy a copy and you will be completely satisfied.